Data Protection from Insider Threats

Synthesis Lectures on Data Management

Editor

M. Tamer Özsu, *University of Waterloo*

Synthesis Lectures on Data Management is edited by Tamer Özsu of the University of Waterloo. The series will publish 50- to 125 page publications on topics pertaining to data management. The scope will largely follow the purview of premier information and computer science conferences, such as ACM SIGMOD, VLDB, ICDE, PODS, ICDT, and ACM KDD. Potential topics include, but not are limited to: query languages, database system architectures, transaction management, data warehousing, XML and databases, data stream systems, wide scale data distribution, multimedia data management, data mining, and related subjects.

Data Protection from Insider Threats
Elisa Bertino
2012

Business Processes: A Database Perspective
Daniel Deutch and Tova Milo
2012

Deep Web Query Interface Understanding and Integration
Eduard C. Dragut, Weiyi Meng, and Clement T. Yu
2012

P2P Techniques for Decentralized Applications
Esther Pacitti, Reza Akbarinia, and Manal El-Dick
2012

Query Answer Authentication
HweeHwa Pang and Kian-Lee Tan
2012

Declarative Networking
Boon Thau Loo and Wenchao Zhou
2012

Full-Text (Substring) Indexes in External Memory
Marina Barsky, Ulrike Stege, and Alex Thomo
2011

Spatial Data Management
Nikos Mamoulis
2011

Database Repairing and Consistent Query Answering
Leopoldo Bertossi
2011

Managing Event Information: Modeling, Retrieval, and Applications
Amarnath Gupta and Ramesh Jain
2011

Fundamentals of Physical Design and Query Compilation
David Toman and Grant Weddell
2011

Methods for Mining and Summarizing Text Conversations
Giuseppe Carenini, Gabriel Murray, and Raymond Ng
2011

Probabilistic Databases
Dan Suciu, Dan Olteanu, Christopher Ré, and Christoph Koch
2011

Peer-to-Peer Data Management
Karl Aberer
2011

Probabilistic Ranking Techniques in Relational Databases
Ihab F. Ilyas and Mohamed A. Soliman
2011

Uncertain Schema Matching
Avigdor Gal
2011

Fundamentals of Object Databases: Object-Oriented and Object-Relational Design
Suzanne W. Dietrich and Susan D. Urban
2010

Advanced Metasearch Engine Technology
Weiyi Meng and Clement T. Yu
2010

Web Page Recommendation Models: Theory and Algorithms
Sule Gündüz-Ögüdücü
2010

Multidimensional Databases and Data Warehousing
Christian S. Jensen, Torben Bach Pedersen, and Christian Thomsen
2010

Database Replication
Bettina Kemme, Ricardo Jimenez-Peris, and Marta Patino-Martinez
2010

Relational and XML Data Exchange
Marcelo Arenas, Pablo Barcelo, Leonid Libkin, and Filip Murlak
2010

User-Centered Data Management
Tiziana Catarci, Alan Dix, Stephen Kimani, and Giuseppe Santucci
2010

Data Stream Management
Lukasz Golab and M. Tamer Özsu
2010

Access Control in Data Management Systems
Elena Ferrari
2010

An Introduction to Duplicate Detection
Felix Naumann and Melanie Herschel
2010

Privacy-Preserving Data Publishing: An Overview
Raymond Chi-Wing Wong and Ada Wai-Chee Fu
2010

Keyword Search in Databases
Jeffrey Xu Yu, Lu Qin, and Lijun Chang
2009

Data Protection from Insider Threats

Elisa Bertino

ISBN: 978-3-031-00762-0   paperback
ISBN: 978-3-031-01890-9   ebook

DOI 10.1007/978-3-031-01890-9

A Publication in the Springer series
SYNTHESIS LECTURES ON DATA MANAGEMENT

Lecture #28
Series Editor: M. Tamer Özsu, *University of Waterloo*
Series ISSN
Synthesis Lectures on Data Management
Print 2153-5418   Electronic 2153-5426

Data Protection from Insider Threats

Elisa Bertino
Purdue University

SYNTHESIS LECTURES ON DATA MANAGEMENT #28

ABSTRACT

As data represent a key asset for today's organizations, the problem of how to protect this data from theft and misuse is at the forefront of these organizations' minds. Even though today several data security techniques are available to protect data and computing infrastructures, many such techniques—such as firewalls and network security tools—are unable to protect data from attacks posed by those working on an organization's "inside." These "insiders" usually have authorized access to relevant information systems, making it extremely challenging to block the misuse of information while still allowing them to do their jobs.

This book discusses several techniques that can provide effective protection against attacks posed by people working on the inside of an organization. Chapter 1 introduces the notion of insider threat and reports some data about data breaches due to insider threats. Chapter 2 covers authentication and access control techniques, and Chapter 3 shows how these general security techniques can be extended and used in the context of protection from insider threats. Chapter 4 addresses anomaly detection techniques that are used to determine anomalies in data accesses by insiders. These anomalies are often indicative of potential insider data attacks and therefore play an important role in protection from these attacks.

Security information and event management (SIEM) tools and fine-grained auditing are discussed in Chapter 5. These tools aim at collecting, analyzing, and correlating—in real-time—any information and event that may be relevant for the security of an organization. As such, they can be a key element in finding a solution to such undesirable insider threats. Chapter 6 goes on to provide a survey of techniques for separation-of-duty (SoD). SoD is an important principle that, when implemented in systems and tools, can strengthen data protection from malicious insiders. However, to date, very few approaches have been proposed for implementing SoD in systems. In Chapter 7, a short survey of a commercial product is presented, which provides different techniques for protection from malicious users with system privileges—such as a DBA in database management systems. Finally, in Chapter 8, the book concludes with a few remarks and additional research directions.

KEYWORDS

data security, data privacy, authentication, access control, anomaly detection, separation-of-duty

I dedicate this book to the many colleagues in academia and industry and to my students who have collaborated with me over the years. Special thanks go to Hal Aldridge, Ji-Won Byun, Elena Ferrari, Ashish Kamra, Murat Kantarcioglu, Gabriel Ghinita, Ninghui Li, Jorge Lobo, Anna C. Squicciarini, Evimaria Terzi, Bhavani Thuraisingham, and James Joshi.

Contents

Acknowledgments xiii

1   Introduction 1
    1.1   A Definition of Insider Threat 2
    1.2   Some Data about Insider Attacks 3
    1.3   Overview of the Lecture 4

2   Authentication 7
    2.1   The Auth-SL System—A System for Flexible, Policy-based Authentication 8
          2.1.1   Reference Architecture 8
          2.1.2   Authentication Policy Language 11
    2.2   Continuous Authentication 12
    2.3   Research Directions 13

3   Access Control 15
    3.1   Access Control Concepts and Models 16
          3.1.1   Access Control Matrix 17
          3.1.2   Mandatory Access Control Matrix 18
          3.1.3   Discretionary Access Control and the System R Access Control Model .. 19
          3.1.4   Role-based Access Control (RBAC) 20
          3.1.5   Attribute-based Access Control (ABAC) 23
    3.2   Content-based Access Control 24
    3.3   Time-based Access Control 27
    3.4   Location-based Access Control 29
    3.5   Purpose-based Access Control 31
    3.6   Usage Control 32
    3.7   Tools for Authoring and Managing Access Control Policies 33
          3.7.1   The SPARCLE System 33
          3.7.2   The EXAM System 34
          3.7.3   Role Mining Tools 35
    3.8   Research Directions 36

4   Anomaly Detection **37**

4.1   Syntax-based Anomaly Detection 39

4.2   Data-based Anomaly Detection.. 41

4.3   Anomaly Response Systems 42

4.4   Research Directions 44

5   Security Information and Event Management and Auditing **47**

5.1   Components of a SIEM Tool 48

5.2   Fine-Grained Auditing 48

5.3   Research Directions 50

6   Separation of Duty **51**

6.1   SoD for Workflow Systems—The BFA Model 52

6.2   The Joint Threshold Administration Model 55

6.3   Proximity Location Constraints 56

6.4   Research Directions 59

7   Case Study—Oracle Database Vault **61**

7.1   Realms 61

7.2   Rule Sets 63

7.3   Command Rules 64

7.4   Multi-Factor Authorization 65

7.5   Separation of Duty 65

7.6   Concluding Remarks 66

8   Conclusion **67**

Bibliography **69**

Author's Biography **77**

Acknowledgments

Parts of the content of this lecture are results of research projects funded by different funding agencies and organizations, including: NSF, AFOSR, DHS, IBM, Sypris Electronics, Northrop Grumman. I would also acknowledge the support of my research provided by Purdue Discovery Park and the constant guidance and support by Dr. Alan Rebar, Executive Director of Discovery Park.

Elisa Bertino
July 2012

CHAPTER 1

Introduction

In today's society, all organizations we may think of rely on data management technologies, such as database management systems (DBMS), for a large variety of tasks, ranging from day-to-day operations to critical decision making. In addition, digital repositories are widely used for storing business-sensitive data, intellectual property (IP), privacy-sensitive data, scientific data resulting from experiments, and so forth. The fact that today we have available an abundance of tools and systems to capture, process, and share huge amounts of data, and sophisticated tools for analyzing and extracting knowledge from very large data sets, is making our society well aware of the value that data have. Recently coined terms like "big data" and "industrial revolution of data" well exemplify that the huge amount of data that organizations have available is making tasks possible that before were impossible, like preventing diseases and crime, personalizing healthcare, quickly identifying business opportunities, managing emergencies, and so on. As discussed by The Economist [2010] *"Managed well, the data can be used to unlock new sources of economic value, provide fresh insights into science and hold governments to account."*

As data has become a key economic resource, its security, privacy, and proper use are crucial requirements. As discussed by Bertino et al. [2011], the proliferation of web-based applications and information systems, and recent trends such as cloud computing and outsourced data management, have further increased the exposure of data and complicated the security problem. As a result, today data security and privacy is an active research and development area in both academia and industry and a wealth of solutions and systems exist that help with well protecting data against external threats. However, as discussed by Shaw et al. [1998], systems including DBMS and applications are designed, configured, and maintained by people, and data are accessed, used, and manipulated by people. As cases described in various reports show [Cappelli et al., 2012; Verizon, 2012], attackers are often individuals, that is, *insiders*, from within the organizations tasked with managing computer systems and data repositories and individuals who have access to data for their carrying on their organizational functions.

The issue of insider threat is inherently a very hard problem to address. Employees in an organization are *trusted* by the organization to carry out its businesses or mission in a professional and legal manner; and thus they possess the necessary authorizations to access much of the organization's proprietary or sensitive data. Such authorizations can easily be misused by malicious or disgruntled employees for a variety of reasons. The threat from such insiders is even greater if they possess super-user privileges to an information system such as the database administrators (DBA) in the case of a DBMS. The problem is further complicated by the fact that today organizational boundaries are very dynamic due to collaborations with partners, contractors, and customers—which often require data sharing.

In what follows, we first elaborate on the notion of insider threat, and then report data about and attacks from insiders. We conclude the chapter with an overview of the subsequent chapters.

1.1   A DEFINITION OF INSIDER THREAT

In order to define the notion of insider threat, we start from the comprehensive definition of malicious insider threat by Cappelli et al. [2012]: *"A malicious insider threat is a current or former employee, contractor, or business partner who has or had authorized access to an organization's network, system, or data and intentionally exceeded or misused that access in a manner that negatively affected the confidentiality, integrity, or availability of the organization's information or information systems."*

This definition emphasizes that malicious insider threats include, in addition to an organization's employees, parties that have collaborations with the organization for various purposes. As of today, data storage and management functions are increasingly being outsourced and offshored or implemented through cloud computing, it is clear that information technology (IT) business partners must be included among potentially malicious insider threats.

Cappelli et al. [2012] also provide an extensive analysis of crimes and identify three main types of crimes:

1. IT sabotage: *"An insider's use of information technology to direct specific harm at an organization or individual."* Examples of sabotage include: destroying critical data, including data backups and copies thus making impossible or extremely expensive to recover the data; planting logical bombs into the system that can trigger data deletion at critical times; and injecting malicious data into control systems, such as those of power grids and manufacturing plants.

2. Theft of IP: *"An insider's use of IT to steal intellectual property from the organization. This category includes industrial espionage involving insiders."* Examples of IP assets that are commonly stolen include: proprietary software, business strategic plans, product details, and customer information.

3. Fraud: *"An insider's use of IT for the unauthorized modification, addition, or deletion of an organization's data (not programs or systems) for personal gain, or theft of information that leads to an identity crime (e.g., identity theft, credit card fraud)."* Examples of frauds perpetrated by misusing data include: submitting false claims to insurances on behalf of innocent customers and having claim payments being routed to addresses different from the ones of the customers, and selling customer data—for example, on the Internet.

The above discussion clearly indicates that almost invariably the target of those crimes is data, which is either disclosed to parties unauthorized for its access, or not used for the organization's intended purposes. In other cases, data are maliciously modified or rendered unavailable when needed by the organization.

It is, however, important to notice that data losses and data security breaches often occur because employees make serious but unintentional mistakes, such as losing laptops, mobile devices, and USB devices that contain sensitive data. The effects of these mistakes can be devastating, as for example, in the well-known case of a U.S. Veterans Affairs employee who took home his laptop along with disks containing records on some 26 million U.S. veterans and had them all stolen out of his home [ITC, 2012]. The reasons for these mistakes can be several, including carelessness, lack of knowledge, difficulties in using security tools, security configuration mistakes, social engineering attacks, and lack of enforcement of organizational policies concerning the context for data use—for example restrictions concerning the locations and devices from which sensitive data can be accessed. We refer to this category of insider threats as *unintentional insider threats.*

The notion of insider threat can now be defined by generalizing the definition of malicious insider threats by Cappelli et al. as follows:

"An insider threat is a current or former employee, contractor, or business partner who has or had authorized access to an organization's network, system, or data and intentionally or accidentally exceeded or misused that access in a manner that negatively affected the confidentiality, integrity, or availability of the organization's information or information systems."

1.2   SOME DATA ABOUT INSIDER ATTACKS

Various organizations have collected data to determine the percentage of insider attacks compared with external attacks. A recent source of data is represented by the CERT CyberSecurity Watch Survey 2011 [CERT, 2011]; this survey reports data about 607 respondents concerning the percentage of respondents that experienced some insider security incident. Data indicate that 21% of security incidents are caused by insider attacks, compared to 58% of security incidents caused by attackers and 21% of security incidents with an unknown cause. Even though the percentage of insider attacks is much lower than external attacks, it is still very significant. It is also important to notice that insider attacks are often considered more costly or damaging to organizations than outsider attacks. The CERT data indicate that 33% of the respondents consider insider attacks more costly or damaging than other attacks compared to 38% that consider outsider attacks more costly or damaging. The data also indicate that the most frequent insider attack is represented by unauthorized access or use of corporate information.

A 2012 report by Verizon [2012] focusing on data breaches gives a very different picture in that this report indicates that the number of outsider attacks grew quite a lot in 2011 due to a major increase in data theft by activist groups—a major new class of data attackers. Consequentially, the percentage of insider attackers in 2011 was a mere 4%. The dataset used to generate the data reported in this report consists of 855 incidents concerning over 174 million of compromised data records. Even though the 2012 Verizon report does not compare its data with the data of the CyberSecurity Watch Survey 2011, the report indicates some reasons for this decrease in insider security incidents. One reason is that data breaches by insiders that resulted in data misuse but not in data disclosure to unauthorized parties were not included in the report. Other reasons pointed out by the report are that insider attacks may go undetected or organizations decide for political reasons to handle them internally and not to report them. An important finding of this report is that even though 90% of the data breaches by insiders were result of deliberate and malicious actions, there were also data breaches resulting from unintentional errors by insiders.

Finally, data about incidents concerning health care information at organizations covered by the US Health Insurance Portability and Accountability Act (HIPAA) of 1996 are available on-line [HHS, 2012]. The data do not indicate whether the breaches were the result of intentional incidents or deliberate actions. However, the data indicate that the cause of many breaches is the theft of portable devices (such as a laptop) on which privacy-sensitive data are stored. Therefore, as already mentioned, it is crucial to protect data not only from malicious insider threats but also from potential unintentional insider threats.

Cappelli et al. [2012] report several real cases of insider attacks showing that in many cases the target of the attack is to steal information or even to create false information. An example of the former is the case of a sale representative of a company who, before moving to a competitor organization, gathered information about customers, business plans, and other proprietary information of the first company. An example of the latter is a case in which a manufacturer company that had outsourced its help desk operations to another company. An employee of the latter company created fictitious customer addresses—corresponding to addresses of relatives—and issued replacement orders from these fictitious customers. Then he sold the received replacement parts for money.

1.3 OVERVIEW OF THE LECTURE

This lecture covers techniques and tools that can help prevent insider threats against data. The focus is thus on technical approaches to the problem. It is, however, important to mention that a comprehensive protection requires also non-technical approaches, such as background checks, anticipating and managing negative issues at workplaces, clearly specifying and enforcing policies concerning accesses, and use of sensitive data. The remainder of the lecture is organized as follows.

Chapter 2 covers authentication techniques. Authentication is a key security technique in that it allows one to verify that a user connecting to a system through a login name is actually the user to whom the login name has been issued to. It is important to remark that insiders are usually authorized to use one or more systems within an organization, and thus have accounts on these systems. Authentication is therefore not a strong protection technique against insider threats. However, fine-grained multi-factor context-based authentication allows one to enforce authentication of different strengths based on the system the user is trying to access and on the context from which the access is being made. Also, stronger authentication provides protection against *masquerading attacks* from insiders. Chapter 3 complements the discussion in Chapter 2 by discussing access control—a fundamental security technique supporting selective accesses to protected resources based on permissions and also on context. By carefully specifying permissions, one can assure that insiders only get access to the data they strictly need, thus minimizing the "attack surface." Moreover, by also restricting accesses based on time and location, one can reduce the attacker's ability to access the data. Chapter 3 thus also covers two very well-known time and location based access control models.

Chapter 4 covers anomaly detection for database accesses. Anomaly detection mechanisms are widely used in intrusion detection systems. They are based on building profiles of normal activity patterns and detecting patterns that are anomalous with respect to these profiles. The application of such mechanisms to databases is crucial for protection from insider threats in that such a mechanism can detect unusual accesses to data that may be indicative of potential attacks. This chapter covers two anomaly detection approaches for databases, based on query syntax profiles and on query result profiles, respectively. Chapter 5 covers logging and auditing tools, including security information and event management (SIEM) tools that are widely used today by organizations in order to collect and manage information and events concerning enterprise security. As such SIEM tools are a key component for insider threat protection and for supporting forensics of data breaches.

Chapter 6 discusses the important security principle of separation-of-duty (SoD), according to which one can prevent frauds and errors by involving more than one individual in the execution of an activity. Techniques implementing SoD can be very effective in protecting against insider threats as their use would force the collusion of several individuals in order to perpetrate the attack. The chapter covers an approach to SoD designed for workflows, and an approach specifically designed for database administrators in the context of an anomaly detection mechanism for a relational DBMS. Finally, Chapter 7 surveys the Oracle Vault product [Oracle, 2012a] which was developed specifically with the goal of protecting from insider threats and enforcing SoD. Chapter 8 concludes the lecture by outlining research directions.

CHAPTER 2

Authentication

Authentication is the process by which systems verify the identity claims of their users. It determines *who* the user is and if his/her claim to a particular identity is true. Authenticated identities are the basis for applying other security mechanisms, such as access control.

Generally speaking, a user can be authenticated on the basis of something he/she holds, he/she is, or he/she knows. *Something you know* is typically implemented through mechanisms such as password, or challenge-response protocols. The *something you hold* approach is implemented through token-based mechanisms, smartcards, or a PIN that the user possesses and must presented in order to be authenticated. Finally, the *who you are* paradigm is based on biometrics and includes techniques such as fingerprint scans, retina scans, voiceprint analysis, and others.

Strong authentication is crucial in protecting users' accounts from being compromised by insiders. For insiders it is easier to steal authentication credentials of colleagues and also to prepare well-crafted phishing attacks, as they are usually aware of habits, preferences, and other information about their colleagues. Also, current authentication approaches have the main drawback of being typically performed only once during the session of a user with a system at the time when the user initially connects to the system. As such, it is not possible to tailor the authentication strength to the specific data that the user is trying to access or to the context from which the access is being performed. Of course, a straightforward solution to authentication for data with different protection requirements is based on a conservative approach that maximizes authentication checks, by requiring for example that the user be authenticated through biometric verification and passwords, each time a user connects to the system. However, such a solution may result in computationally consuming authentication tasks and may also be very expensive and complex to deploy. For example, adopting one-time passwords for all users of an organization, independently from the tasks they have to perform and the data they have to access, may be very expensive; ideally, one would like to require such authentication measures only for users who need to access sensitive data and use conventional passwords for the other users. It is thus important not only that authentication is based on a variety of mechanisms, but also that it be easily configurable based on the actions the users are trying to perform, and also be continuous, that is, not limited to a specific time during a session.

It is also important to notice that authentication is part of the broad area of *identity management* [Bertino and Takahashi, 2010]. Identity management refers to the set processes and tools supporting the management of identity information about users in a system, including the creation and deletion of user accounts, the issuance and verification of authentication credentials, like passwords or smart cards, the management and verification of security-relevant information about users. It is crucial that all such processes and tools, in addition to being highly secure, also to be properly managed so as to promptly and correctly modify identity information according to changes in the organizational structure and user population and functions. Some data thefts that were reported occurred because organizations did not revoke accounts of users that had left the organizations, thus allowing these users to still access the organization's data. Current centralized digital identity management systems are addressing some of these issues by, for example, centralizing the management of all users' accounts. As such, comprehensive and well-governed digital identity management is a crucial component of any solution to the problem of insider threat. We refer the reader to the text by Bertino and Takahashi [2010] for a comprehensive discussion of concepts, standards, and research issues in the area of digital identity management.

In the reminder of this chapter we focus on approaches that are critical for protection against insider threats. We start by a presentation of Auth-SL, a flexible approach for authentication based on the notion of authentication policies (Section 2.1.) The presentation follows the content of the paper by Squicciarini et al. [2007]. We then present approaches for continuous authentication (Section 2.2). We conclude the chapter by a discussion on research directions (Section 2.3).

2.1   THE AUTH-SL SYSTEM—A SYSTEM FOR FLEXIBLE, POLICY-BASED AUTHENTICATION

Auth-SL system was developed with the goal of supporting authentication solutions based on the use of multiple authentication mechanisms combined through *authentication policies* and on the association of the authentication policies with the protected resources. Authentication policies are expressed through a special purpose *authentication language*, also implemented as part of Auth-SL. It is important to emphasize that Auth-SL departs from the conventional security "pipeline" according to which, during a user session with a system, authentication is executed only once at the beginning of the session, and then access control is applied multiple times during the session. Auth-SL is based on a different paradigm under which the activities of authentication and access control can be interleaved in a session, depending on the specific security requirements of the resources accessed during the session. It is important to note that the conventional security pipeline can be supported in Auth-SL as a special case.

In what follows, we first present the reference architecture of Auth-SL and then present the authentication policy language. An implementation of Auth-SL has been developed as part of the FreeBSD Unix operating system. We refer the readers to [Squicciarini et al., 2007] for a discussion on implementation issues and performance results.

2.1.1   REFERENCE ARCHITECTURE

Auth-SL consists of two major subsystems, namely the *authoring subsystem* and the *enforcement subsystem* (see Figure 2.1).

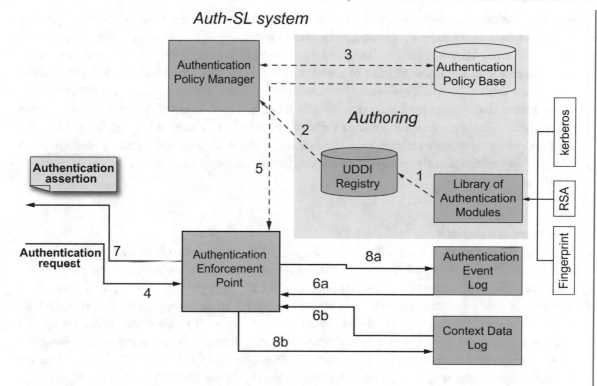

Figure 2.1: The Reference Architecture for a policy-based.

Authoring Subsystem

This system supports the specification and the management of the authentication policies (Steps 1, 2, and 3 in Figure 2.1). One of its key features is that it supports the specification of which mechanism to use through the specification of conditions against the features of the available mechanisms. Such specification relies on two components: a *library of authentication modules*, each implementing a specific authentication function; and a specialized *UDDI Registry* recording all features of the authentication modules that are relevant for the specification of the authentication policies. Each module in the library supports a specific type of authentication. Such modules can then be dynamically invoked to enforce the specific authentication policies. The information required about the authentication modules that is needed for authoring authentication policies (Step 3 in Figure 2.1) is as follows. (1) *Module's authentication characteristics.* These data describe the settings for the specific mechanism. For example, in a password based authentication, a characteristic is the maximum number of authentication attempts allowed, or the minimum length of the password. For token-based authentication, a characteristic is the authentication method (e.g., single-sign-on Basic-Auth credentials), credentials (username, password, domain), and X.509 client certificates, and the software used (e.g., IBM Tivoli Client RSA). (2) *Implementation data.* These parameters qualify the specific implementation of a mechanism and can refer to the storage of the secret token, the cryptographic technique used to transmit it, the audit trails, and so forth.

The authentication policies that can be expressed thus depend on the authentication modules available, and the characteristics of these modules. Such data are to be considered part of the knowledge needed to specify adequate authentication policies. For example, if a system administrator knows that a given authentication module is weak, due to implementation limits or module vulnerabilities, he/she can apply stronger authentication policies. Authored authentication policies are stored in a repository referred to as *Authentication Policy Base* providing query capabilities to properly authorized users, such as system administrators and auditors.

Enforcement Subsystem

Upon an authentication request (Step 4 in Figure 2.1), such a system is in charge of evaluating an authentication policy and making an *authentication decision*. The evaluation is executed by the *Authentication Enforcement Point*, which first retrieves a proper authentication policy (Step 5 in Figure 2.1). Policy evaluation may also take into account previous *authentication events* concerning the subject being authenticated. To express fine-grained constraints over past authentications the system collects information on the past authentication in two different logs, serving different purposes: (i) track subject's actions related to authentication (Steps 6.a and 6.b in Figure 2.1); and (ii) record the conditions under which a successful authentication is executed (Step 8.a and 8.b in Figure 2.1). The first log, referred to as *Authentication event log*, records authentication events (*event* for short) related to the subjects. An authentication event is basically an authentication executed against a subject. Such log tracks in a chronological order all events related with user authentication performed during each session. Once the policy is evaluated, a new event is generated and stored in the log in order to keep track of this authentication step. Each record can refer to either an authentication attempt using a specific factor, the verification, and/or the failure of the verification of a given factor. A successful authentication implies successful authentication of multiple factors traced in the event log. The *context data log* instead tracks specific data related to previous authentication. The information stored by such log is used to evaluate whether previously executed authentication can be leveraged for satisfying an authentication policy. An instance of the context data log is created when the user begins a session and it is maintained only for the session duration. Each log record stores context data related to the specific authentication performed, and the settings of the module used. Each entry of such log records: the type of mechanism used, the time of the authentication execution, the number of failed attempts, the party that originally generated the authentication token used, storage information (remote vs. local token storage), and the storage mode (encrypted vs. clear text token).

The output of the enforcement subsystem is an authentication assertion, which can be either returned to the user or transmitted to some other system or application (Step 7 in Figure 2.1). Since policies are associated with resources, in most cases the authentication service will interact with the access control system. Typically, when a subject requires access to a resource, the access control system requires the authentication service to determine if there are authentication policies associated with the resource, and, if this is the case, to evaluate such policies.

2.1.2   AUTHENTICATION POLICY LANGUAGE

Authentication policies are the key elements to drive authentication decisions. The specification of authentication policies relies on the notion of *Authentication Factor*. Authentication factors define the features of a specific authentication, where by *authentication* we intend the execution of one authentication protocol using a single mechanism (that is, the "factor"). Authentication factors are specified in terms one or more *descriptor*. A descriptor is basically a predicate expressing a property required for the authentication factor. An example of authentication factor specified by two descriptors is

$$\{\text{Mechanism} = \text{Biometrics}, \text{Feature} = \text{Fingerprint}\}.$$

The first descriptor requires that the authentication be based on the use of a biometric authentication mechanism, whereas the second descriptor specifies that the feature used in the biometric authentication must be the fingerprint. All the properties characterizing an authentication module are recorded in the UDDI registry and they can be referenced in descriptors. Additional types of descriptor are related to contextual information, such as space and time, and to the issuers and verifiers of authentication tokens. Temporal descriptors are used in particular to specify "freshness conditions" concerning authentication; these conditions specify how recent an authentication factor must be.

The authentication factors, as defined above, are stand alone in that the specification of one single factor is not related to other factors. However, this is not adequate for the specification of complex and multi-factor authentication policies. To correlate different factors and their characteristics, constraints can be specified; we refer to these constraints as *factor constraints*. In Auth-SL, factor constraints are specified as logic formulae in which the occurring variables are the factor identifiers.

The previous elements, that is, authentication factors and factor constraints, are combined into the notion of *authentication policy*. Such a policy is composed of five elements: (i) a protected object O and a set S of operations defined on O; (ii) a list of authentication factors $[f_1, \ldots, f_k]$; (iii) an *order* flag; (iv) a *threshold* value; and (v) a set of factor constraints. As it can be noticed, a policy is associated with an object and one or more operations defined on the object; this means that the authentication specified by the policy must be executed whenever one such operation is executed on the object. The specification of multiple authentication factors expresses multi-factor authentication policies. The listed factors may or may not all be mandatory, as specified by the threshold value; for example a policy may specify a list of five authentication factors, of which only three must be verified by the subject being authenticated. Additionally, the execution order of various authentication factors may or may not have relevance. If the order according to which factors should be evaluated is significant, then the *order* flag is set to *yes*. The listed factors are to be evaluated accordingly. If order is set to *no*, the factor evaluation order is not mandated.

As an example, consider the authentication policy $< file1, \{open\}, \text{TRUE}, [f_1, f_2, f_3], 3, \varphi >$ where

$f_1 = Mechanism(z_1, Biometric) \wedge Algorithm(z_1, VeriFinger)$ is an authentication factor requiring a biometric authentication through fingerprint;

$f_2 = Mechanism(z_2, Kerberos)$ is an authentication factor requiring an authentication through a Kerberos ticket;

$f_3 = Mechanism(z_3, Password)$ is an authentication factor requiring an authentication through a password;

$\varphi = Issuer(f_2) \neq Issuer(f_3)$ requires that the issuer of the password and the Kerberos ticket be two different parties.

This policy states that in order to be authenticated for opening *file*1 the user identity should be checked by executing factors f_1, f_2, f_3 according to this order.

The specification of the ordering and the mandatory number of factors enhances the flexibility and the expressive power of the policy language. The order can be specified according to the relevance of the factors, or their sensitivity, or the cost for their verification. Thus, it can help in optimizing the usage of system resources. Similarly, the specification of the threshold enhances the flexibility of authentication by establishing the sufficient demands needed to authenticate the user.

2.2   CONTINUOUS AUTHENTICATION

Continuous authentication is motivated by the need of addressing the shortcomings of conventional authentication approaches that only authenticate the users at the beginning of the user's session with the system. The main idea is that a user should continuously be authenticated while interacting with the system. An important requirement is that the authentication be passive as an authentication system that would continuously require the user to authenticate would have low usability. To address such requirement, the use of behavioral biometrics has been proposed [Yampolskiy and Govindaraju, 2008]. Unlike physiological biometrics that relies on physical traits of individuals, like fingerprints, behavioral biometrics is based on behavioral traits exhibited by users when interacting with a computer system. Yampolskiy and Govindaraju [2008] identified five different categories of behavioral biometrics. Of these categories, the most relevant category, is represented by the human-computer interaction (HCI)-based biometrics. More specifically, HCI-based biometrics is based on the observation of the human interaction with input devices such as keyboards, computer mice, and haptics which can register inherent, distinctive and consistent muscle actions. One can thus create a profile of such interactions for each user and determine at run-time whether the behavior exhibited by a user matches his/her HCI-based biometric profile. One advantage of HCI-based behavioral biometrics compared with physiological biometrics is that the latter requires biometrics sensors to be available at the user machine, whereas the former does not have such requirement. Also, the latter is not passive in that it may require the user to perform some specific actions, whereas the former supports passive authentication.

Among the HCI-based biometrics, the most well-known approaches are based on keystroke dynamics for password hardening [Monrose et al., 1999] and on mouse movements [Zheng et al., 2011]. The keystroke dynamics approach requires an attacker not only to have to know the password of the victim user, but also to type it as the legitimate user would do in order to successfully impersonate the victim. This approach, however, has been used only in the context of password-based authentication mechanism and not for continuous authentication, whereas the mouse movement approach has the more general goal of continuously authentication users. Also, as discussed by Zheng et al. [2011], the keystroke dynamics approach requires the authentication system to record sensitive textual information, whereas the mouse movement approach does not have this shortcoming. A critical issue of both approaches is represented by the fact that the user biometrics may change depending on the device used and the context in which the user is located. Also, whether the mouse movement approach provides strong authentication is still under debate; assessments concerning this issue have been carried out experimentally and thus until more extensive experimental analyses are carried out it is too early to make definite conclusions.

2.3   RESEARCH DIRECTIONS

Strong authentication is crucial for preventing impersonation attacks from insiders, especially from insiders that have system privileges and are thus able to get access to authentication credentials of other users in their organizations. It is, however, important to notice that a single authentication mechanism may not be sufficient or adequate in all circumstances. Thus, needs authentication systems able to support and combine different authentication mechanisms, ranging from conventional password-based mechanisms to behavioral biometrics, also based on the data the user is trying to access or modify and on the user context. In this respect, an interesting research direction is how to combine the policy-based authentication system described in Section 2.1 with behavioral authentication. Here, a difficult challenge is represented by the integration of behavioral authentication with operating systems and DBMS.

CHAPTER 3

Access Control

Access control is a key component of any security solution for protecting against insider threats. Access control determines which subjects can access which data under which circumstances and thus allows one to make sure that users can only access data according to their job responsibility. As a consequence, data exposure is reduced.

From a conceptual point of view, an access control mechanism is organized as shown in Figure 3.1 [Bertino, 2012]. An access control mechanism typically includes a reference monitor that checks that requested accesses by *subjects* to protected *objects* to perform certain actions on these objects are allowed according to the access control policies. The decision taken by the access control mechanism is referred to as *access control decision*. Of course, in order to be effective for protection from insider threats, access control mechanisms must support fine-grained access control that refers to finely tuning the permitted accesses along different dimensions, including data object contents, time and location of the access, purpose of the access. By properly restricting the contexts of the possible accesses one can reduce the opportunities for insiders to steal data. To address such a requirement, extended access control models, have been proposed that we survey in this chapter. It is also important to notice that fine-grained access control requires specifying fine-grained access control policies which are used by the reference monitor to take access control decisions. The specification of such policies may not be trivial and therefore tools and techniques have been proposed to generate and analyze such policies.

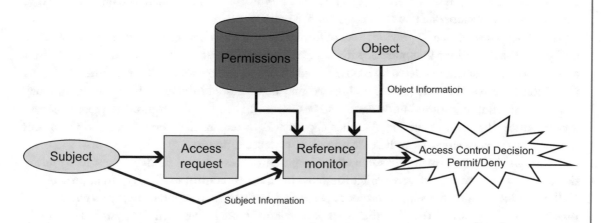

Figure 3.1: A generic access control mechanism architecture [Bertino, 2012].

In this chapter, we first survey basic notions concerning access control models (Section 3.1), including the well-known RBAC model, and recent attribute-based access control models. We then discuss support for content-based access control according to which access decisions are conditioned to the actual content of the data objects (Section 3.2). We then present (Sections 3.3, 3.4, and 3.5) an overview of three extended access control models, that support time-based access control, location-based access control, and purpose-based access control, respectively. We then briefly discuss the usage control model (Section 3.6), which represents an important generalization of the notion of access control with important applications to the problem of insider threats. We conclude the chapter by a discussion on tools for the specification and analysis of access control policies (Section 3.7). Finally, we outline some research directions (Section 3.8).

The presentation in this chapter is partially based on the chapter by Bertino [2012] and the chapter by Bertino and Crampton [2007]. We also refer the reader to Bertino et al. [2011] for a detailed coverage of access control systems for DBMS.

3.1   ACCESS CONTROL CONCEPTS AND MODELS

The organization of access control (see Figure 3.1) suggests that there is an active subject requiring access to a passive protected object to perform some operation [Lampson, 1974]. A reference monitor permits or denies access. The reference monitor consults permissions and/or information about the subject and the object or their relationship in order to decide about the access request. Subjects typically include users, but also application programs and processes running on behalf of users. Typical information used about subjects and objects in access control is their system identifiers. Advanced access control models, however, extend this basic information with a large variety of information about the subjects and objects, thus resulting in the so-called *attribute-based access control models*, and with contextual information, such as time and location. We refer to an access control system as a system comprising of a reference monitor, and all information required for taking access control decisions, such as the access control policies.

An *access control model* provides a set of formal constructs for encoding an access control policy and states the conditions that must be satisfied for an access request to be granted. In other words, it provides the conceptual model to be implemented by the access control mechanism. The conditions that determine whether a request is authorized may be expressed in many different ways and may require evaluating additional information. One approach is to simply require the presence of an authorization that permits access. Another approach is to require that the subject and the object have certain relationships, as in the case of mandatory access control.

In what follows, we survey some of the important access control models. We start by introducing the access control matrix which the most basic access control model. We then present the Bell-LaPadula model, the most representative model in the area of mandatory access control. We proceed with a survey of the discretionary access control model developed for System R, an early DBMS prototype based on the SQL language. We then cover the well-known RBAC model. We conclude with a discussion on recent attribute-based access control models.

3.1.1   ACCESS CONTROL MATRIX

The *protection matrix,* the first theoretical access control model [Harrison et al., 1976], is an abstract representation of permissions specifying the access requests that are authorized. A protection matrix is a two-dimensional array, with each row labeled by a subject and each column labeled by an object. A matrix entry in the row labeled s and column labeled o specifies the authorized actions (also called *access rights*) for s with respect to o. For example, a matrix entry for s and o that contains *write* specifies that subject s is allowed to write object o. In other words, the protection matrix encodes triples of the form subject-object-action (referred to as *authorizations*); object-action pairs are often referred to as *permissions* or *capabilities*. The protection matrix model also includes operations for its manipulations, namely for entering and deleting actions from the matrix entries, and for adding and deleting subjects and objects. Such operations are collectively often referred to as the model for *access control administration*. Efficient and effective administration models are crucial.

Even though one may use a protection matrix in order to implement an access control system, actual access control systems rarely adopt the protection matrix for storing authorization information. This is because in a computer system with many subjects and objects, the memory requirements for the protection matrix would be prohibitively large. Also, such a matrix is typically sparse as in most cases each subject can only access a small subset of the protected objects and thus most entries in the matrix would be empty. Alternative approaches to the efficient implementation of the protection matrix are based on the use a set of *access control lists* or *capability lists*. These structures have the feature that only relevant matrix entries are stored, with empty matrix entries being ignored. An access control list is associated with an object and consists of a number of entries defining the rights assigned to each subject for that object. In contrast, a capability list is associated with a subject. Conceptually, a capability list is a list of permissions; each such permission identifies an object and the rights that have been assigned to the subject for that object. In other words, each permission in a capability list for a subject specifies how that subject may interact with the object specified in the permission.

Approaches based on access control lists have been further enhanced in order to reduce the size of access control lists and the administration costs. Reducing administration costs is crucial in contexts that require fine-grained authorization as in the case of protection from insider threats. Relevant extensions to reduce administrative costs include the use of groups and the use of negative authorizations. The idea of groups is that certain permissions can be assigned with a single administration command to a group. Each subject who is a member of the group *implicitly* receives the permissions assigned to the group. A subject may be associated with a number of different groups, and in more advanced group models, a group can be a member of another group. Negative authorizations explicitly prohibit certain actions by certain subjects on certain objects. They are particularly useful for enforcing exceptions to a more general permission. For example, suppose we wish to grant read permission to a subject on all files in a directory except for one file f. If the directory contains a huge number of files, without the use of negative authorizations, we would need to grant the subject an authorization for each file, thus resulting in a large number of administration operations. A less burdensome way to implement the previous access control requirement would be to grant the subject a general permission to read all files in the directory and then specify a negative authorization on f. Under such an approach only two administration operations would be required. The notion of negative authorization was initially proposed as part of the Orion authorization model [Rabitti et al., 1991] and adopted by various systems and models, including the OASIS eXtensible Access Control Markup Language (XACML) standard[1].

3.1.2   MANDATORY ACCESS CONTROL MATRIX

Unlike the access control models based on the notion of access control matrix, in the mandatory access control access control decisions are based on specific relationships between the subject requesting access and the object to which access is requested. An important motivation for the mandatory access control is to control the flow of information once information has been accessed. Access control mechanisms based on the notion of access control matrix typically only control whether each single access is authorized; however, they do not control where the data flows once it has been accessed. As such, access control mechanisms are unable to protect against "Trojan Horses." A "Trojan Horse" is a piece of code embedded into an application program. When the program is running on behalf of a subject, the "Trojan Horse" exploits the authorizations of this subject in order to gain access to protected data and transfer the data into some other objects accessible to subjects not authorized to access the protected data. Access control mechanisms based on the mandatory access control prevent such attacks.

The most well-known mandatory access control model is the Bell and LaPadula (BLP) model [Bell and LaPadula, 1976]. Under a mandatory access control model, the action of accessing a data object starts an information flow. In particular, reading a data object causes information to flow from the data object to the subject, while the flow is in the opposite direction if the subject writes to the data object. A mandatory access control model thus consists of rules specifying which information flows are authorized.

In the BLP model the information flows are authorized based on comparing a certain specific property of subjects and data objects. This property, referred to as *access class*, is associated with each subject and data object. The access class of a data object indicates the sensitivity of the data object, whereas the access class of the subject indicates how much the subject can be trusted not to disclose sensitive information.

Each access class consists of two elements, and the set of all access classes is partially ordered according to a relation called *dominance relation*, denoted by $\geq$. Accesses to data objects by subjects are regulated by two properties.

1. The simple security property (*no-read-up*): a subject can read a data object if its access class dominates the access class of the data object.

---

[1] http://www.oasis-open.org/committees/tc_home.php?wg_abbrev=xacml

2. The *-property (*no-write-down*): a subject can write into a data object if its access class is dominated by the access class of the data object.

For a system to be secure both properties must be verified by any system state.

This model has been implemented in several systems, including operating systems and DBMSs. A notable example is represented by Oracle Label Security, a relational DBMS product in which access classes, called *labels*, consist of three components and which also provides a comprehensive environment for the management of labels and associations of labels with data objects and users.

3.1.3   DISCRETIONARY ACCESS CONTROL AND THE SYSTEM R ACCESS CONTROL MODEL

Even though there is no unique definition of the notion of discretionary access control, we can say that such notion is used to characterize context in which certain users are able to control permissions to access the protected objects. These users can enter at their discretion permissions or access control rules allowing accesses to the objects. The most common implementations of discretionary access control are based on the notion of object *owner*; the owner of an object is usually the creator of the object and controls the permissions associated with the object. Variations are, however, possible as discussed in detail by Bertino and Ferrari [1998].

A significant implementation of discretionary access control has been in the context of the System R relational DBMS prototype [Astrahan et al., 1976] that we discuss in what follows. In addition to extending the basic notion of discretionary access control with an authorization administration delegation mechanism, System R also introduced an approach to support content-based access control. Such form of access control requires that access control decisions be based on the content of the data objects. The System R access control model has been further extended with different types of authorization revocation and negative authorizations [Bertino et al., 1999b].

In the system R access control model the main protected objects are the relations, storing data, and the authorized actions correspond to the SQL operations that can be executed on the relations. Such actions include: `select` (to retrieve tuple from a relation), `insert` (to insert tuples into a relation), `delete` (to remove tuples from a relation), and `update` (to modify tuples in a relation). The update authorized action can be further refined by specifying the relation columns to which it applies. Therefore, a user may receive the privilege to modify only a subset of the columns of a relation.

Authorization administration in System R is based on the ownership approach extended with authorization administration delegation. Under the ownership approach, when a user creates a new relation, the user becomes the owner of the relation and is solely and fully authorized to exercise all actions on the relation. The owner can further delegate privileges on the relation to other subjects by granting these subjects authorizations with the grant option. The command for granting authorizations, introduced by System R, is the `GRANT` command. Its basic format is as follows. In the command syntax the curly brackets denote a set of alternative elements of the command, one of which must always be included in the command, whereas the square brackets denote optional components of the command.

```
GRANT {ALL PRIVILEGES|  <privileges >} ON  <table>
TO {<user-list> | PUBLIC} [WITH GRANT OPTION]
```

The ALL PRIVILEGES and PUBLIC keywords denote the set of all access rights and all users, respectively. The WITH GRANT OPTION keyword specifies that the user receiving the privileges specified by the command, that is, the *grantee*, receives also the administration authorization on these privileges and can thus grant them to other users. The user issuing a GRANT command is referred to as the *grantor* of the authorizations. The following are examples of the use of the grant command. In the example commands the name before the character ":" denotes the grantor.

- Mary: GRANT select, insert ON Employee TO Jim WITH GRANT OPTION;

- Mary: GRANT select ON Employee TO Bob WITH GRANT OPTION;

- Jim: GRANT select, insert ON Employee TO Bob;

It is important to notice that as results of execution of the above GRANT commands, user Bob has the select privilege (granted by both Mary and Jim) and the insert privilege (received from Jim). Bob in turn can grant to other users the select privilege because he has received it with the grant option; however, he cannot grant the insert privilege.

Authorizations can be dynamically revoked through the REVOKE command. An important principle stated by the System R model is that a user can revoke an authorization only if the user is the grantee of this authorization. The format of the REVOKE command is as follows:

```
REVOKE {ALL PRIVILEGES|  <privileges >} ON <table>
FROM {<user-list> | PUBLIC}
```

Note that as a user may receive the same privilege from multiple grantors, because of decentralized administration, the execution of a revoke operation does not necessarily result in the user loosing the privilege. We refer the reader to the paper by Griffiths and Wade [1976] for details about the semantics and implementation of the revoke operation in the System R access control mechanism.

3.1.4   ROLE-BASED ACCESS CONTROL (RBAC)

The main motivation for role-based access control (RBAC) is to reduce authorization administration costs. In access control systems based on conventional access control, like control based on access control lists, the number of authorizations can be very high. For example, in a system with 1,000 users, 100,000 objects and 10 access rights, there are 10^9 possible authorizations. Moreover, if the user population is highly dynamic, the number of grant and revoke operations to be performed can become very difficult to manage. RBAC addresses such problems by introducing the concept of a *role*, which acts as an intermediary between users and permissions (see Figure 3.2). The idea is that there will be far fewer roles than either users or permissions and also the set of roles in an organization is relatively more static that the set of users. An important positive side effect of the use of roles is that permissions are granted to roles, instead than to users; as such, permissions are expressed at a higher level of abstraction and this contributes to simplify the specification, analysis, and management of access control policies and enhances the process of verifying the posture of organizations with respect to access control. Because of these reasons, RBAC has been standardized [ANSI, 2004] and has been implemented in a large number of systems, from operating systems to DBMSs, and also as part of identity management systems. RBAC has also been the subject of extensive research, which we briefly discuss after introducing the basic elements of RBAC.

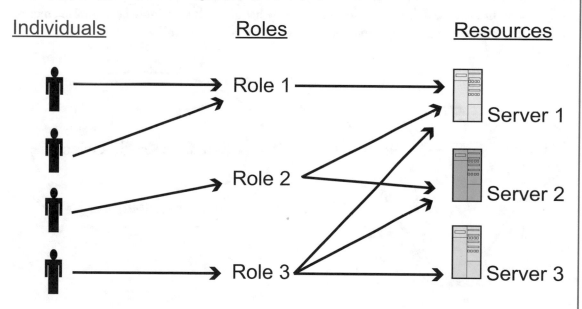

Figure 3.2: Users change frequently, roles are stable.

The basic concepts of RBAC are illustrated in Figure 3.3. As shown by the figure, RBAC is defined in terms of several sets: a set of users U, a set of permissions P and a set of roles R. A user is human being, and a role represents a job function or job title within the organization with some associated semantics regarding the authority and responsibility conferred on a member of the role. In an academic context, examples of roles are student, professor, staff, president, provost, and so forth. A permission is usually assumed to be an object–action pair; the specific types and formats of permissions depend on the system in which RBAC is deployed. When used to control accesses to a relational SQL database, the objects are the relations and other database objects, whereas the actions correspond to SQL commands, such as SELECT and INSERT. Users are associated with roles using a user-role assignment relation UA. This relation is a set of pairs of the form (u, r), meaning that user u is assigned to role r. Permissions are granted to roles and revoked from roles.

The permission-role assignment relation *PA* indicates which permission is assigned to which role. A user thus receives all the permissions granted to the roles that have been assigned to the user.

Users interact with an RBAC system by activating a session. A session is defined as "a mapping between a user and an activated subset of roles that are assigned to the user" [ANSI, 2004] and it is thus quite abstract. An example of a session in the context of an RBAC-based access control mechanism for a database system is a database transaction. Typically, the user authenticates to the DBMS and chooses to act in one or more of the roles to which he is assigned. If *s* makes an access request for permission *P* during the session, the permissions of the session roles are considered. If the requested permission is among them, the access request is granted. In general, not many implementations of RBAC support sessions, mainly because it is a notion whose implementation highly depends on the actual system adopting RBAC for access control.

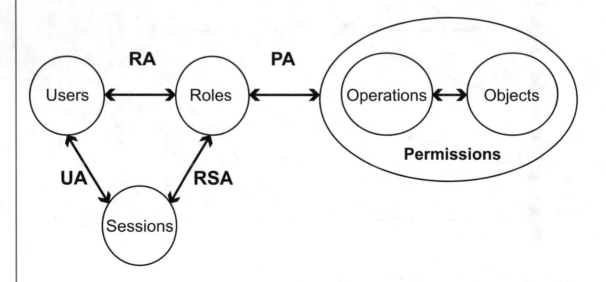

Figure 3.3: The components of the basic RBAC model.

RBAC further reduces the administrative cost by using the notion of *role hierarchy*, that is, a directed acyclic graph in which the nodes represent the roles. The basic idea of the role hierarchy is that a role high up in the hierarchy will inherit the permissions of lower roles, without having to be explicitly assigned those permissions. Clearly, this significantly reduces the number of permissions that need to be assigned to more senior roles, thereby reducing the administrative overhead. Such an approach, however, introduces an overhead into the access control checking algorithm, because it is necessary to consider the permissions of all junior roles when making an access control decision.

3.1.5   ATTRIBUTE-BASED ACCESS CONTROL (ABAC)

Attribute-based access control (ABAC) is based on the idea of characterizing subjects and objects by sets of attributes, encoding security-relevant properties of the subjects and objects, and then denoting subjects and objects in authorizations by conditions on these attributes. Therefore, a subject can access an object if an authorization A exists such that the subject verifies the subject conditions in A and the object verifies the object conditions in A. An example of an ABAC authorization is the authorization stating that "MPEG movies for adults can be downloaded only by users with age equal or greater than 18 years." Such authorization does not indicate any specific user identifiers, such as login names. Rather, it implicitly applies to all users whose age verifies the condition of being equal or higher than 18. Similarly, the protected objects are not indicated by specifying their names, such as file names; they are denoted by the predicate "category = for adults." ABAC thus relies on the use of attributes that describe the subjects and the protected objects. The use of ABAC has the main advantages of providing a high-level approach for specifying authorizations so that authorizations can more easily be derived from organizational security policies. As such, it makes easy the fine-tuning of authorizations for the purpose of protection from insider threats.

XACML is a well-known model based on the notion of ABAC and has been developed for addressing the need of collaborative data sharing across different organizational domains for which an expressive attribute-based access control model is a key requirement. XACML is an extensible, XML-encoded language, for specifying access control policies, access requests, and access control decisions. Its main features can be summarized as follows.

- It is based on authorizations expressed as triples of the form: ⟨Resource, Subject, Action ⟩. (The term "Resource" is the one adopted by XACML to mean "protected object"). Each entity in such a triple can be specified by using an identifier for the entity or specifying a set of conditions against some attributes associated with the entity. As such XML is an ABAC model.

- It supports a structured organization of access control policies. Basically, the top element of an XACML policy is a set of policies, each of which aggregates other policy sets or *policy elements*. The main component of a policy element is the notion of *rule set*, consisting of multiple rules, that is, of multiple triple-based authorizations.

- It supports negative authorizations and provides different algorithms for solving conflicting access control decisions resulting from different rules (e.g., rule-combining algorithms) and different policies (e.g., policy-combining algorithm). A rule encoding a negative authorization has the Effect component set to "Deny," whereas for positive authorizations the Effect component is set to "Permit."

- It is extensible. The elements of XACML that can be extended include: functions, identifiers, data types, rule-combining algorithms, and policy-combining algorithms.

The following is an example of an XACML policy:

```
<Policy ID = P1>
<Target>
     <Subjects> <Subject> GroupName = IBMOpenCollaboration </Subject>
</Subjects>
     </Target>
<Rule ID = R11 Effect = Permit>
     <Target>
          <Subjects> <Subject> Designation = Professor </Subject>
</Subjects>
          <Resources> <Resource> FileType = Source </Resource>
</Resources>
          <Actions> <Action> Type = Read </Action> </Actions>
          <Environments> <Environment> Time = (8AM, 6PM)
</Environment> </Environments>
     </Target>
     <Condition> (FileSize < 100MB) </Condition>
</Rule>
<Rule ID = R12 ..> ... . </Rule>
```

In XACML, a key notion is the notion of policy representing a single access control policy, expressed through a set of rules. A rule specifies the *target* to which it applies and the *effect* of the rule; that is, Permit or Deny. The target basically models the access request, by means of a set of simplified conditions for the subject, resource and action that must be met, i.e., evaluate to the Boolean value true, for the rule to apply to a given request. In other words, the target of a rule specifies the set of requests to which the rule is applicable; such specification is intensionally expressed by a set of conditions. Any number of rule elements may be used, each of which generates a true or false outcome. Combining these outcomes results in a single decision for the policy, which may be a Permit, Deny, Indeterminate, or a NotApplicable decision. A decision may also contain some obligations, that is, actions, which must be executed once the subject has obtained access to the data. Examples of obligations include logging information about the accessed data or notifying an individual that his/her personal data have been accessed.

3.2   CONTENT-BASED ACCESS CONTROL

Content-based access control places conditions on accesses to the protected data objects based the contents of these objects. An example of a content-based access control policy would be the policy stating that "data concerning salaries equal or greater than 200K can only be accessed by the manager of the HR division, whereas data concerning salaries lower than 200K can be accessed by the manager of the HR division or one of his/her deputies." Under this policy, if one such deputy issues a query to retrieve all data concerning employees working in a given project, the access control system has to check whether the returned data verifies such condition. In case some of these data do not verify this condition (e.g., the data refer to employees with a salary equal or greater than 200K), the access control system has to deny access to this specific data.

Content-based access control is crucial for protection against insider threats in that it allows one to clearly identify data that are sensitive because of their contents and thus limit the access to these data. However, the actual implementation of content-based access control is not trivial in that it requires an approach by which content conditions can be specified. In relational DBMSs, such a mechanism is typically based on declarative query conditions expressed in SQL. Such an approach has the advantage that when data content changes, if the new version of the data verifies the conditions of an access control policy, the system is able to automatically enforce this policy.

The first proposed approach for content-based access control in relational DBMS is based on the use of the view mechanism [Bertino and Haas, 1988; Bertino et al., 1983; Griffiths and Wade, 1976]. The view mechanism allows one to define "virtual relations" consisting of subsets of columns and/or tuples of relations defined by using queries—these queries are referred to as *view definition queries*. For example, one can define a view that only selects from an employee relation the tuples having salary lower than 200K. Views thus define dynamic windows based on query conditions on the underlying relations. Views can be queried very much like conventional relations. When processing a query on a view, the DBMS combines the conditions expressed in the query on the view with the conditions in the view query definition. As such, the conditions specified on the view are used to filter out certain data; in our example of a view selecting employee data with salary lower than 200K, the view will filter out any employee data for employees with salary equal or greater than 200K. If users are granted access to a view, the users when querying the view will never receive the data filtered out by the view.

The view mechanism has however the major problem that when different content-based access control policies must be enforced on the same table for different users, one needs to create as many views as these access control policies and then make sure that each user is authorized to use only the correct view. Such an approach complicates the application programs as each application program then needs to include application logics to check with view to use to query a given relation depending on the user on behalf of whom the program is running. To address such issue, a different approach, implemented by the Oracle DBMS, is based on transparent query re-writing. The main idea is that when a user issues a query on a given table, the DBMS transparently (to the user) re-writes the query by appending to the query additional conditions filtering out the data that the user cannot see. The issue for this approach is how to define such conditions. In Oracle, this is achieved by the Virtual Private Database (VPD) mechanism [Oracle, 2012b]. A VPD is associated with a table and its main component is represented by a policy function. Such policy function implements the required access control policy for the associated table and, when evaluated, it returns an SQL condition. The evaluation occurs at each query invocation and the returned SQL condition is appended to the query, thus making sure that the data returned by the query is filtered according to the policy. A large variety of parameters are available to the policy function at run-time, including the current user, that is, the user who has issued the query being processed, and the role being used by this user (if any), whether the user is database administrator, and so on. An example of a policy function is reported in Figure 3.2(a) for a table called `emp_table` consisting of two columns with names "owner" and "data," respectively. This function implements a policy stating that "users can only access data that refers to them; however DBAs should be able to access any data without restrictions." In the policy definition, `userenv` is a pre-defined application context, `object_name` is the name of table or view to which the policy will apply, and `object_schema` is the schema owning the table or view. Figure 3.2(b) shows the definition of a VPD that associates this policy function with the `emp_table` table. Suppose now that user Bob, who is not a DBA, issues the query ``Select * from emp_table;.'' The query is transparently re-written as ``Select * from emp_table where owner = 'Bob';''.

```
Create  function  sec_function  (object_schema  varchar2,  object_name
varchar2)
Return varchar2
As
     user VARCHAR2(100);
Begin
     if ( SYS_CONTEXT('userenv', 'ISDBA') ) then
           return ' ';
     else
           user := SYS_CONTEXT('userenv', 'SESSION_USER');
           return 'owner = ' || user;
     end if;
End;
```

(a) An example of a policy function.

```
      execute dbms_rls.add_policy (object_schema => 'Alice',
            object_name => 'emp_table',
            policy_name => 'my_policy',
            function_schema => 'Alice',
            policy_function => 'sec_function',
            statement_types => 'select, update, insert',
            update_check => TRUE );
```

Figure 3.4: (b) Associating the policy function in Figure 3.2(a) with table `emp_table`.

Oracle VPD is a powerful mechanism as it allows one to enforce a large variety of access control policies, including past accesses performed by the users if this information is logged by the DBMS or applications. Its main drawback is that access control policies are not declaratively expressed as they are expressed as code in policy functions. Such an approach makes very difficult to determine whether the implemented policies comply with high level organizational policies. Also changing the policies requires modifying the code of these functions which makes security maintenance expensive.

3.3   TIME-BASED ACCESS CONTROL

An important requirement for fine-grained access control mechanisms in the context of protection from insider threats is related to the temporal dimension of permissions. It is important that authorizations given to users be tailored to the pattern of their activities within the organization. Therefore, users must be given access authorizations to data only for the time periods in which they are expected to need the data. An example of a time-restricted policy is that "The system administrator in charge of performing the back-up of the project files can only access the files Friday afternoons between 3 pm and 6 pm;" this policy strictly limits the time that the administrator has for accessing the files and thus reducing the opportunities for him/her to steal data.

An expressive authorization model addressing the above requirements is by Bertino et al. [1998]; this model introduces the notion of non-periodic and periodic authorization and supports both positive authorizations (e.g., authorizations granting permissions) and negative authorizations (e.g., authorizations denying accesses—useful for supporting authorization exceptions). Another relevant feature of this model is the possibility of specifying derivation rules expressing temporal dependencies among authorizations. These rules allow the derivation of new authorizations based on the presence or absence of other authorizations in specific periods of time. By using derivation rules, many protection requirements can be concisely and clearly specified. For example, it is possible to specify that two users, working on the same project, must receive the same authorizations on certain types of objects; or that a user should receive the authorization to access an object in certain periods, only if nobody else was ever authorized to access the same object in any instant within those periods. Derivation rules are specified by constraining the rule application with a temporal expression, by providing the authorization to be derived, by specifying one of the three temporal dependency operators that the model provides, and, finally, by giving the body of the rule in the form of a Boolean expression of authorizations. The three temporal dependency operators correspond to the three main temporal relations among authorizations that have been identified in common protection requirements.

More in detail, the authorization notions of this model are based on the following definitions [Bertino et al., 1998].

Definition (Authorization). Let U be a set of users, O be a set of protected objects, M a set of actions that can be executed on the objects in O. *An authorization* is defined as a 5-tuple (s, o, m, pn, g) where $s, g \in U, o \in O, m \in M$, and $pn \in \{+, -\}$.

In the above definition, s denotes the user to whom the authorization is granted, whereas g denotes the user who granted this authorization to s. In this respect, this model follows the decentralized authorization administration model of System R. Also, authorizations can be positive, denoted by the $+$ sign in the last component, or negative, denoted by the—sign in the last component.

Definition (Periodic Authorization). A *periodic authorization* is a triple ([*begin, end*], P, *auth*), where *begin* is a date expression, *end* is either the constant ∞, or a date expression denoting an instant greater than or equal to the one denoted by *begin*, P is a periodic temporal expression, and *auth* is an authorization (defined according to the previous definition).

The periodic authorization ($[begin, end]$, P, (s, o, m, pn, g)), states that authorization (s, o, m, pn, g) is granted for each time instant in temporal periods denoted by P that is greater than or equal to the instant denoted by *begin* and smaller than or equal to the instant denoted by *end*. For example, the periodic authorization ([1/1/04, 12/31/06], Mondays, (Matt, o1, read, +, Bob)), granted by Bob, states that Matt has the authorization to read object o1 each Monday starting from 1/1/04 until 12/31/06. Periodic authorizations in which the upper date *end* is equal to ∞ are valid until explicitly revoked by a REVOKE command. A non-periodic temporal authorization is an authorization in which the periodic temporal expression P is missing. For example, the authorization ([1/1/04, 12/31/06], (Matt, o1, read, +, Bob)) states that Bob can read object o1 at any time between 1/1/04 and 12/31/06.

Definition (Derivation rule). A *derivation rule* is a triple ($[begin, end]$, P, $A < OP > \mathcal{A}$), where $\overline{begin}$ is a date expression, *end* is either the constant ∞ or a date expression denoting an instant greater than or equal to the one denoted by *begin*, P is a periodic expression, A is an authorization, $\mathcal{A}$ is a Boolean expression of authorizations, and $< OP >$ is one of the operators: WHENEVER, ASLONGAS, UPON.

Like authorizations, each derivation rule has a bounding time interval and a periodicity, representing the instants at which it can be applied. The three derivation operators have been selected in order to express three intuitive temporal relations among authorizations. The derivation of new authorizations is obtained with WHENEVER by considering authorizations valid in the same time instants, and with ASLONGAS by considering the validity of authorizations in a whole span of time, whereas UPON allows the expression of *triggering* conditions. The following examples illustrate the derivation rules. In the example rule we assume that all authorizations are issued by the same subject (e.g., Sam).

The rule
([2012, 2013], Working-days, (part-time-staff, *, read, +, Sam) WHENEVER (staff, *, *, +, Sam) ∨ (temporary-staff, *, read, +, Sam))
states that part-time-staff can read, in any instant of a working day in the period [2012–2013], any object (denoted by the * symbol) on which either temporary-staff has read privilege or staff has any privilege, for that instant.

The rule
([2012, 2013], Working-days, (temporary-staff, document, read, +, Sam) ASLONGAS (summer-staff, document, read, +1, Sam))
states that temporary-staff can read any document in each working day in the period [2012, 2013] until the first working day in which summer-staff will be allowed for that.

The rule
([2012, 2013], Working-days, (Ann, pay-checks, read, +, Sam) UPON (Tom, pay-checks, write, + Sam))

states that Ann can read the pay-check data object each working day starting from the first day in the period [2012–2013] in which Tom can write the pay-checks data object.

Notice that as these derivation rules are based on the notion of deriving authorizations from other authorizations, the process of authorization derivation is a recursive process. When checking an access request, the authorization monitor has to determine whether the requested authorization is an explicit authorization, that is, an authorization explicitly granted, or can be derived from the explicitly granted authorizations from the recursive application of derivation rules. To formally express the semantics of the authorization derivation model, this temporal authorization model has been formally defined by using the Datalog deductive database language extended with nonmonotonic negation, periodicity, and gap-order constraints on the integers. We refer the reader to Bertino et al. [1998] for details on such formal model.

The notion of temporal constraints has also been applied to the RBAC model, resulting in the well-known temporal-RBAC (TRBAC) model [Bertino et al., 2001]. TRBAC constrains the use of permissions assigned to roles to specific temporal periods. Therefore, even though a user has the permission to use a role, and thus to use all the permissions assigned to this role, the user may only use the role in specified temporal intervals, which can also be periodic (for example, "every Tuesday from 10 am to 5 pm"). TRBAC thus extends RBAC with the association of temporal (possibly periodic) intervals with roles. In TRBAC roles can be in two mutually exclusive states: active state, which is the state in which the role can be used; and non-active state, which is the state in which the role cannot be used. Typically, a role is in the non-active state at all times outside the temporal interval associated with the role.

In addition, TRBAC provides the notion of dependencies among role activation/de-activation, expressed by means of role triggers, whose actions may be either executed immediately, or be deferred by an explicitly specified amount of time. A trigger allows one to specify for example that whenever a role is activated, another role must be activated. Therefore, the events that can be specified in TRBAC triggers refer to role activations and deactivations, and actions consist of activating and de-activating roles. Both triggers and periodic activations/deactivations may have a priority associated with them, in order to resolve conflicting actions. Conflicting actions may result from the execution of multiple triggers, as in the case of database triggers. A formal semantics for TRBAC has been defined, and a polynomial safeness check has been introduced to reject ambiguous or inconsistent specifications.

3.4   LOCATION-BASED ACCESS CONTROL

Location is an important dimension with respect to the secure use of data. Organizations often require that sensitive data are only accessed at the their premises; such limitations ensure that such data are only accessed in environments that are more secure with respect to both cyber security and physical security. With respect to protection from insider threats, location-restricted access control is crucial in several respects. Environments in which access is permitted may implement stronger security, such as video surveillance cameras recording actions users are making. Such an approach may allow one to detect if users are taking pictures of the screen on which data are displayed. If a malicious insider is trying to impersonate another user, a location constraint imposing that accesses be performed only from the office of the latter user would require the former user to gain access to such office, which will then make the attack very difficult.

In a location-based access control, authorizations include an additional parameter specifying the location in which the access granted by the authorization is allowed. As in temporal access control, in location-based access control, an authorization is not active, that is, it cannot be used, unless the user is located in the location specified in the authorization. The definition and implementation of location-based access control requires addressing two major issues. The first is the definition of a model for expressing locations. The second is the definition and deployment of mechanisms for high-assurance detection of user locations Bertino and Kirkpatrick [2011b]. As a location-based access control relies on determining the user position in order to make access control decisions, it is crucial that such position be trustworthy.

The GEO-RBAC model [Damiani et al., 2007] is an access control model addressing the first issue. It is based on the notion of a *spatial role* that is, a geographically bounded organizational function. The boundary of a role is defined as a geographical feature, such as a road, a city, or a hospital, and specifies the *spatial extent*, that is, a region in a reference space of interest, in which the user has to be located in order to use the role. Thus, a spatial role is defined as a pair $\langle r, e \rangle$, where r is the role name and e the spatial extent (extent for short) of the role. The geometric representation (geometry) adopted by GEO-RBAC is compliant with the OGC (Open GeoSpatial Consortium) *simple-feature* geometric model [OpenGIS, 1999]. In such a model, the geometry of an object can be of type point, line or polygon, or recursively be a collection of disjoint geometries. A point describes a single location in the coordinate space; a line represents a linear interpolation of an ordered sequence of points; a polygon is defined as an ordered sequence of closed lines defining the exterior and interior boundaries of an area. An interior boundary defines a hole in the polygon. As it is reasonable to assume that the extent of a role has, besides a geometric representation, a semantic characterization, in GEO-RBAC role extents are semantically modeled as spatial features. Spatial features are identified by names and refer to entities that can be mapped onto locations in the reference space; the locations are represented through a geometry. Thus, in GEO-RBAC, the extent associated with the role can be specified as a spatial feature. An example of role definition in GEO-RBAC is: ⟨ doctor-St.Elizabeth, St.Elizabeth-Hospital ⟩. This definition specifies a role, whose name is doctor-St.Elizabeth, and whose extent is the St. Elizabeth Hospital; therefore, any permission granted to this role can only be used when the user using this role is located inside the St. Elizabeth Hospital. Notice that in many application domains, one may need to specify more general policies; in the context of a healthcare application domain, one may specify the policy that "Doctors associated with a hospital can only use authorizations on medical data when they are in the hospital." To support such requirement, GEO-RBAC provides the notion of *role schema* by which one can specify such policies. In such role schema, instead of using a specific feature, for example a specific hospital, ones use a spatial feature type, that is, a type that generalizes a set of similar spatial features. Examples of spatial feature types are hospital, city, lake. Roles can then be derived from these role schemas by instantiating a specific spatial feature from the spatial feature types used in the schemas. An example of a role schema is ⟨Doctor, Hospital ⟩. In addition, GEO-RBAC also supports the notion of role hierarchies and spatial feature hierarchies and constraints supporting mutual exclusion of roles within the same access session. We refer the reader to Damiani et al. [2007] for additional details and formal definition of GEO-RBAC.

Concerning the second issue, a possible approach is based on the use of Near Field Communication (NFC) technologies [Kirkpatrick and Bertino, 2010]. NFC is an RFID-based proximity-constrained technology that provides contactless communication between a device and a reader/writer. In contrast to traditional one-way RFID mechanisms, NFC has a number of advantages. NFC has a very restricted broadcast range, typically 10 cm, which helps to create a stronger assurance of the user's location. NFC also defines a peer-to-peer mode that exchanges data in both directions in a single contactless session. This mode mitigates the threat of passive attacks that steal data stored in NDEF tags [Madlmayr et al., 2008]. Under such NFC-based approach, each location of interest, that is, a location corresponding to a role extent, must be equipped with a location device that securely stores a certificate storing the location device identifier and the location coordinates. The certificate is signed by the role manager, that is, a centralized component in charge of managing roles. Whenever a user needs to use a spatial role, the user interacts with the location device associated with the extent of the role to obtain a cryptographic hash that binds the user with the location of the device. Such hash is then submitted to the access control monitor by the user together with the access request and allows the user to prove his/her location to the access control monitor. As the NFC technology requires that the user be located in very close proximity to the location device, this provides a strong guarantee of the user location. Notice, however, that as users may move after obtaining the access, one may have to continuously monitor the user location and different approaches are possible. In closed environments, for example, in order to leave the location associated with a role (for example a room), the user can be required to unlock a door using again NFC–based protocol which would then de-activate the role, or the user may be required to periodically prove his/her location.

3.5   PURPOSE-BASED ACCESS CONTROL

An important aspect in access control policies for the protection of privacy-sensitive data are represented by the *purpose of data use*. Many regulations and privacy policies explicitly mention the purpose for which collected personal data are used. A policy may specify for example that address data of customers is collected only for the purpose of shipping the products ordered by the customers. Incorporating the notion of purpose into an access control system is crucial for protection from insider threat as the purpose confines the use of data to very specific tasks that the users accessing the data carry on. Therefore, any use of the data outside the intended tasks can be flagged as anomaly and triggers additional on-line checks and verification of the user activities.

An access control model explicitly incorporating the notion of purpose has been defined by Byun et al. [2004, 2005]. This model is based on the notion of intended purposes, which specify the intended usage of data, and access purposes, which specify the purposes for which a given data element is accessed. Both intended purposes and access purposes are specified with respect to a hierarchical structure organizing a set of purposes for a given organization A key feature of this model is that it also supports explicit prohibitions, thus allowing security officers to specify that data should not be used for a given set of purposes. Purposes are organized into a purpose tree that allows one to use a hierarchical approach for defining and refining the purposes of interest. A key issue in the application of such model is the granularity of purpose labeling, that is, the data elements with which purpose information are associated. Byun et al. [2004] identified four different levels, that is, relation, relation column, tuple, tuple field, and investigated strategies based on bitmap techniques, for efficiently encoding and storing fine-grained purpose information (e.g., at the tuple level and the tuple field level). Experimental results show that a factor impacting the query performance is the number of columns accessed by the queries; also the experiments show that for large data size the overhead introduced by the storage and checking of purpose information is minimal.

An important issue in the above model and more general in the use of purpose-based access control is how to determine the access purpose, that is, the reason why a user is accessing a certain data object. The above model assumes that the access purpose is declared as part of the query and thus the model includes an extended format for SQL queries supporting the specification of access purpose. However, such an approach relies on the user and/or the application program to provide such information and therefore it may not be effective against malicious insiders. A stronger different approach would require profiling the different activities of the users and associate purposes with these profiles. Therefore, whenever a user would perform an activity, the activity would be matched against the activity profiles to determine the profile matching the activity; then the purpose associated with the activity would be associated with each data access request issued by the user when executing the activity. Thus, only the data accesses consistent with the purpose of the activity would be allowed. To date, however, approaches like this one have not yet been explored.

3.6   USAGE CONTROL

A critical limitation of conventional access control models is that access control is performed before the access is executed. Once the access is allowed, no other controls or actions are executed by the access control system. However, applications such as digital right management (DRM) require that the usage of the protected objects is also controlled; for example, one may want to prevent a user from copying an object to which the user has obtained access. Also, a subject may incur some obligations once he/she has accessed an object; for example the subject must inform the owner of a protected object about how the data object has been used. Such requirements call for a comprehensive approach to controlling protected data objects even after access to them has been granted. Such a comprehensive approach fits very well with the requirements of protection from insider threats, as being able to control how data objects are used once they are accessed would help preventing many malicious actions.

A comprehensive usage model, known as $UCON_{ABC}$, has been proposed [Park and Sandhu, 2004] that includes not only authorizations, but also obligations and conditions. The model thus subsumes access control in that it covers also obligations, that is, requirements that have to be fulfilled by subjects before or after the access, and conditions, that is, subject and object-independent environmental or system requirements that have to be satisfied for access. The model also covers the notions of continuity (ongoing controls) and mutability. Mutability refers to changes to the subjects and/or the objects that arise after access has been granted and may require changes to the access control decision while the access is being made. An example of mutability is represented by changes in the location of user in location-based access control after the access has been granted. Depending on the policy, one may still allow the access or may drop it.

The $UCON_{ABC}$ model has established some very interesting principles for generalizing access control and is a model that subsumes many other models, including location and time based access control models. Its main drawback is that certain aspects of the model and of the corresponding enforcement engine are application-dependent and thus implementation and deployment of $UCON_{ABC}$ would require an extensible architecture. An extensible approach to obligation management has been recently proposed [Li et al., 2012]. One open research direction is how to generalize such approach to fully support $UCON_{ABC}$.

3.7 TOOLS FOR AUTHORING AND MANAGING ACCESS CONTROL POLICIES

As access control systems are increasingly being deployed and the complexity of the access control models and authorization languages is increasing, tools for the authoring and analysis of access control policies are crucial. Such analyses are quite complex when dealing with models like XACML in which policies have complex structures and are based on subject and object attributes. Also, as advanced access control models, like RBAC, are deployed, there is also the need of tools able to automatically extract high-level policies from low-level authorizations, such as permission lists. In what follows, we survey some of the tools that have been proposed. We start with tools for authoring, analyzing, and integrating access control policies with reference to two well-known systems: SPARCLE and EXAM. Then we survey tools for role mining; these are tools able to automatically generate roles of an RBAC system by mining low-level permissions existing in the system of interest.

3.7.1 THE SPARCLE SYSTEM

The SPARCLE system [Karat et al., 2005] was developed with the goal of supporting privacy policy authoring by users with a variety of number of skills, ranging from lawyers and business process specialists to security experts and information technologists. To address such goals, SPARCLE allows individuals responsible for policy authoring to specify the policies by using a guided natural language or a structured format. Policies entered in natural language are parsed by a shallow natural language parser and automatically translated into a machine-readable format. The structured format allows users to select from a number of menus driving the specification of the policy elements. The menus are related to various components of the policies, such as purposes, conditions, and obligations. Policies specified according to the structured format are then mapped onto the machine-readable format. SPARCLE also generates a natural language representation for the policies specified in the structured format and a structured representation for the policies entered in natural language. Therefore, each policy in SPARCLE has three representations which are kept synchronized: natural language, structured format, machine-readable format. At any time when authoring and editing policies, users can switch between the natural language representation and the structured format. SPARCLE has been assessed by user studies with respect to the readability of the policies created. The assessment has shown that the readability of policies authored by the guided natural language and the structured format is higher that the readability of policies authored in free natural language. We refer the reader to Karat et al. [2005] for details and a comprehensive tour of the SPARCLE user interfaces.

3.7.2   THE EXAM SYSTEM

The EXAM system has been developed with the goal of supporting different types of analysis and integration of attribute-based access control policies, including policies expressed in XACML [Lin et al., 2010]. EXAM consists of four main components.

- The **Policy annotator** preprocesses each policy by adding annotations to it. The annotations explicitly represent the behavior or semantics of each function referred in the policy. Such annotations help in automatically translating policies into Boolean formulae that can then be evaluated by the policy analysis modules.

- The **Policy filter** [Lin et al., 2007] evaluates the similarity of a pair of policies and assigns the pair a similarity score ranging from 0–1. The higher the similarity score, the more similar are the two policies. The similarity function implemented by the policy filter is based on similarity techniques proposed in the area of information retrieval and it is very efficient. An example of two policies and the similarity measure assigned to these two policies by the policy filter is shown in Figure 3.5.

- The **Policy similarity analyzer (PSA)** module is the core component of EXAM. Given two policies, it supports two types of queries.

  - Common property query: this query determines the set of requests that are authorized by both policies.

  - Discrimination query: this query determines the set of requests that are authorized by one policy and denied by the other policy.

    The technique implementing these queries is based on the use of the multi-terminal binary decision diagram (MTBDD) [Fisler et al., 2005] combined with the policy ratification technique by Agrawal et al. [2005]. EXAM also supports a sophisticated visualization environment, based on a multi-level grid visualization technique, for showing the results of the queries to the user. We refer the reader to Lin et al. [2010] for details about the analysis algorithms and their performance.

- The **Policy integration framework** supports the integration of policies using operators defined as part the fine grained integration algebra (FIA) [Rao et al., 2009]. It uses the MTBDD based representation of policies to implement the algebraic operators. Operations on policies are mapped onto operations on the corresponding policy MTBDDs and an integrated policy MTBDD is obtained. The integrated policy MTBDD is then traversed to generate a well-formed XACML version the integrated policy.

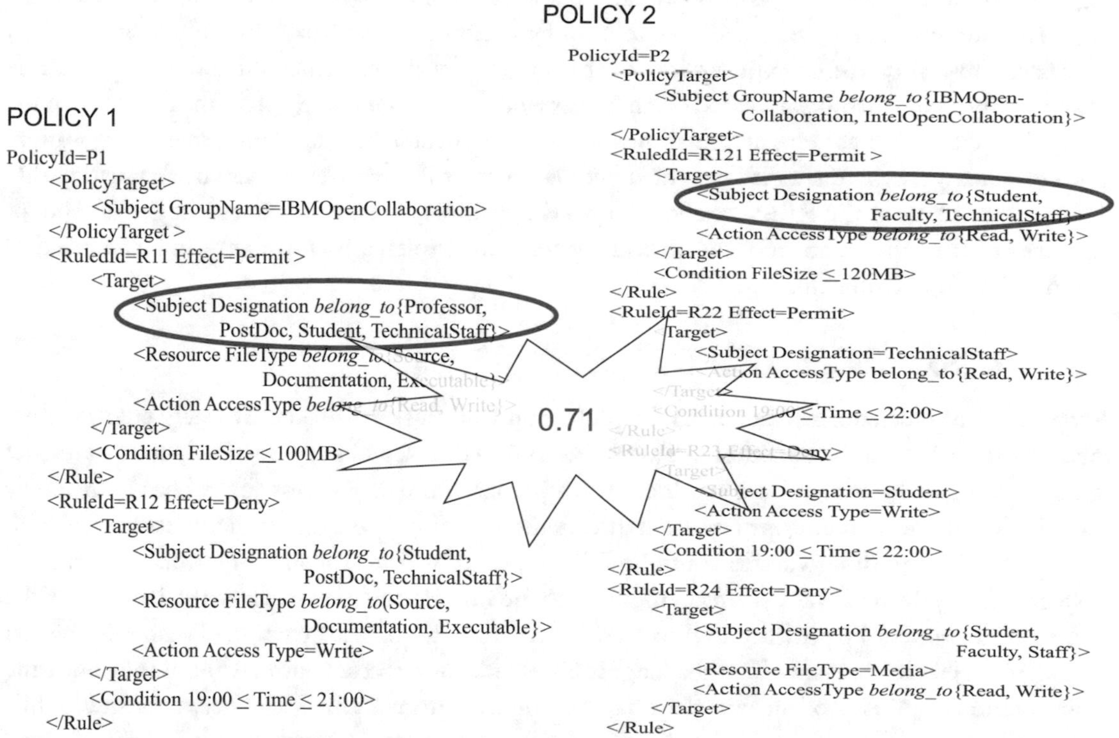

POLICY 2

POLICY 1

```
PolicyId=P2
  <PolicyTarget>
    <Subject GroupName belong_to{IBMOpen-
              Collaboration, IntelOpenCollaboration}>
  </PolicyTarget>
  <RuledId=R121 Effect=Permit >
    <Target>
      <Subject Designation belong_to{Student,
                Faculty, TechnicalStaff}>
      <Action AccessType belong_to{Read, Write}>
    </Target>
    <Condition FileSize ≤ 120MB>
  </Rule>
  <RuleId=R22 Effect=Permit>
    Target>
      <Subject Designation=TechnicalStaff>
      Action AccessType belong_to{Read, Write}>
    </Target>
    <Condition 19:00 ≤ Time ≤ 22:00>
  </Rule>
  <RuleId=R23 Effect=Deny>
    Target>
      <Subject Designation=Student>
      <Action Access Type=Write>
    </Target>
    <Condition 19:00 ≤ Time ≤ 22:00>
  </Rule>
  <RuleId=R24 Effect=Deny>
    <Target>
      <Subject Designation belong_to{Student,
                Faculty, Staff}>
      <Resource FileType=Media>
      <Action AccessType belong_to{Read, Write}>
    </Target>
  </Rule>
```

```
PolicyId=P1
  <PolicyTarget>
    <Subject GroupName=IBMOpenCollaboration>
  </PolicyTarget >
  <RuledId=R11 Effect=Permit >
    <Target>
      <Subject Designation belong_to{Professor,
                PostDoc, Student, TechnicalStaff}>
      <Resource FileType belong_to{Source,
                Documentation, Executable}>
      <Action AccessType belong_to{Read, Write}>
    </Target>
    <Condition FileSize ≤ 100MB>
  </Rule>
  <RuleId=R12 Effect=Deny>
    <Target>
      <Subject Designation belong_to{Student,
                PostDoc, TechnicalStaff}>
      <Resource FileType belong_to(Source,
                Documentation, Executable}>
      <Action Access Type=Write>
    </Target>
    <Condition 19:00 ≤ Time ≤ 21:00>
  </Rule>
```

0.71

Figure 3.5: An example of application of the policy similarity.

3.7.3   ROLE MINING TOOLS

The development of tools for role mining has been motivated by the fact that, as pointed out by Molloy et al. [2010], creating an RBAC configuration from scratch is not easy and this is the most expensive task when migrating to an RBAC system. Two approaches have been identified for creating RBAC configuration. The first is a *top-down approach* and consists of performing a detailed analysis of the business workflows within the organization of interest and deriving the RBAC configuration from this analysis. This approach requires extensive human involvements and it is thus very expensive. The *bottom-up* approach addresses such shortcoming by automatically deriving roles from existing system configuration data through role mining. It is important to mention that those two approaches are not mutually exclusive and they can be used in combination.

Role mining has attracted considerable interest from the research community and role mining techniques have been proposed [Molloy et al., 2010; Vaidya et al., 2006]. As discussed by Molloy et al. [2010], most approaches do not address the problem of discovering roles which have a semantic meaning, that is, that have some correspondence with actual functions within the organization of interest. Also, they do not address which role configuration to select, as when mining roles, one can came up with different role configurations. The approach by Molloy et al. [2010] addresses those shortcomings. It introduces the notion of weighed structural complexity of a role configuration; such complexity, based on an earlier work by Bertino et al. [2003], measures the number of elements, such as roles and relationships that are included in the mined role configuration. The complexity measure is called weighted because giving different weights can be assigned to different components of the RBAC configurations. For example, if one wants to reduce the number of instances of the inheritance relationship among the mined roles, a high weight can be assigned to the inheritance relationship.

3.8   RESEARCH DIRECTIONS

Access control mechanisms are crucial for protection from insider threats. By finely tailoring permissions according to the data contents as well as to the context and purpose of use, one can restrict the opportunities for data misuse and theft. Even though the area of access control has been widely investigated, there are many open research directions, including how to reconcile access control with privacy, and how to design access control models and mechanisms for social networks and mobile devices. Many advanced access control models require that information, such as the location of the user requiring access, be provided to the access control monitor. The acquisition of such information may result in privacy breaches. The challenge is how to perform access control while at the same time maintaining the privacy of the user personal and context information. Social networks and mobile devices acquire a large variety of information about individuals; therefore access control mechanisms are needed to control with which parties this information is shared. The main issue is that, unlike conventional enterprise environments in which administrators and other specialized staff are in charge of authoring access control policies, in social networks and mobile devices end-users are in charge of authoring their own personal access control policies. The main challenge is thus the design of easy-to-use approaches and tools supporting end-user policy authoring and automatically revisions of these policies based also on end-user feedback.

CHAPTER 4

Anomaly Detection

As discussed by Chandola et al. [2009] *"anomaly detection refers to the problem of finding patterns in data that do not conform to expected behavior."* In computer security, anomaly detection techniques have been traditionally applied to intrusion detection, that is, to detect break-ins by attackers external to the protected system. As intrusions are typically characterized by different behaviors than normal activities, anomaly detection techniques represent a well suited defense technique against intrusions.

A more recent and interesting application of anomaly detection is in the protection of data from insider threats. The main idea is to profile the normal behaviors of insiders with respect to data access, and then to detect insider behavior that is anomalous with respect to the normal behaviors. As discussed by Mathew et al. [2010], anomaly detection is mostly effective for protecting against non-stealthy attacks, such as quick data harvesting attacks and masquerading attacks, as these attacks would have profiles significantly different from the normal insider activities.

The application of anomaly detection techniques to database systems requires addressing several issues.

- How to profile the database accesses. Profiles typically consist of features characterizing the data accesses; examples of features include the syntax of queries and statistical summaries of query results. It is crucial that the feature extraction process as well as the comparison with the profiles of normal behavior be very efficient as anomaly detection must be executed at run-time for each query issued to the system.

- Where to locate the anomaly detection engine. Most solutions, especially commercial ones, use monitor tools that reside at the network level and check for SQL commands. Such solutions have good performance; however they are ineffective against insiders, as often insiders like DBA directly connect to the database. Other solutions are based on analyzing log files, recording all database activities, for detecting anomalous accesses. However, such solutions are able to detect the anomalies only after the accesses have been completed and therefore unable to block the data accesses in time. A better approach is based on locating the anomaly detection engine at the database server and possibly integrating with the database engine. Such an approach has excellent performance and is able to detect anomalous data accesses before queries are executed.

- How to respond to the detected anomalies. Automatic response to anomalies is crucial for the usability of an anomaly detection system as we cannot expect that each anomaly be manually handled by some system administrator or DBA. A possible approach is to allow the system administrator or DBA to specify the actions to be taken when an anomaly is detected based on information such as the access context. To date, however, this is an aspect that has not been much investigated.

Figure 4.1 provides a high-level view of a reference architecture of an anomaly detection system, based on the approaches by Kamra et al. [Kamra and Bertino, 2010; Kamra et al., 2008], illustrating the various components of such system and their inter-relationships.

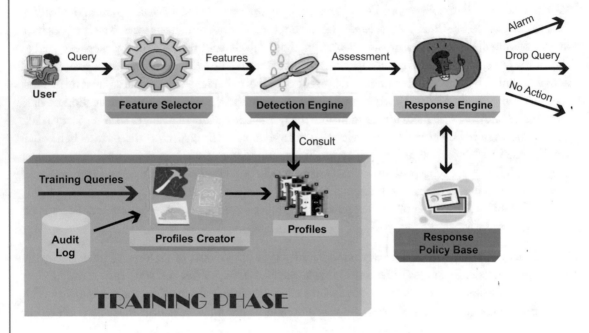

Figure 4.1: Reference architecture for an Anomaly Detection System.

In the reminder of this chapter we discuss in more detail various aspects of anomaly detection systems for databases. In what follows, we first present (Section 4.1) a syntax-based anomaly detection system proposed by Kamra et al. [2008] as this system has been the first anomaly detection system developed for relational DBMS and among its features it provides support for user roles. From an architectural point of view, this system is based on an anomaly detection engine located inside the DBMS; the actual implementation of this system has extended the PostGres DBMS with the anomaly detection system. We then survey (Section 4.2) an approach by Mathew et al. [2010] which characterizes the data accesses by statistics on the data returned by queries. We then present (Section 4.3) an approach to the problem of anomaly response by Kamra and Bertino [2011], which to date is the only existing approach to the automatic management of anomalies. We conclude the chapter by a discussion of research directions (Section 4.4).

4.1   SYNTAX-BASED ANOMALY DETECTION

In a syntax-based anomaly detection mechanism, profiles of data accesses consist of features extracted from the issued queries. Of course a large number of possibilities exist when dealing with which features to extract from queries, ranging from very minimal information (like just the query command) to detailed information about the query predicates. When minimal information is collected, the accuracy of anomaly detection is typically very low; however, the impact on performance is minimal. By contrast, when detailed information is collected the accuracy is good but performance is heavily impacted. To address such issue, Kamra et al. [2008] defined and evaluated three different representations:

1. **Coarse quiplet (c-quiplet** for short): A representation that includes the command used in the query, the number of tables and attributes used in the projection clause of the query, and the number of tables and attributes used in the qualification clause (that is, the WHERE clause) of the query. This representation thus consists of five fields (SQL-CMD, PROJ-RELCOUNTER, PROJ-ATTR-COUNTER, SEL-REL-COUNTER, SEL-ATTR-COUNTER). The first field is symbolic and corresponds to the issued SQL command. The next two fields are numeric, and correspond to the number of relations and attributes involved in the projection clause of the SQL query. The last two fields are also numeric, and correspond to the number of relations and attributes involved in the selection clause of the SQL query.

2. **Medium quiplet (m-quiplet** for short): A representation that extends the c-quiplet representation by indicating which tables are used in the project clause of the query and which tables are used in the qualification clause of the query. For each such table, the representation only encodes the number of attributes used from the table, but not the names of these attributes. This representation thus consists of five fields (SQL-CMD, PROJ-REL-BIN[], PROJ-ATTR-COUNTER[], SEL-REL-BIN[], SEL-ATTR-COUNTER[]). The first field is symbolic and corresponds to the issued SQL command; the second is a binary (bit) vector of size equal to the number of relations in the database. The bit at position i is set to 1 if the ith relation is projected in the SQL query. The third field of the quiplet is a vector of size equal to the number of relations in the database. The i-th element of the PROJ-ATTR-COUNTER[] vector corresponds to the number of attributes of the i-th relation that are projected in the SQL query. The semantics of SEL-REL-BIN[] and SEL-ATTR-COUNTER[] vectors are equivalent to those of PROJ-REL-BIN[] and PROJ-ATTR-COUNTER[] vectors, but the information kept in the former corresponds to the selections rather than to the projections of the SQL query.

3. **Fine quiplet (f-quiplet** for short): A representation that extends the m-quiplet representation by indicating not only which tables are used in the query, but also the names of these attributes. As with the previous representations, this representation distinguishes between the tables and the attributes used in the projection clause of the query, and the ones used in the qualification clause of the query. This representation thus consists of five fields (SQL-CMD, PROJ-REL-BIN[], PROJ-ATTR-BIN[][], SEL-REL-BIN[], SEL-ATTR-BIN[][]). The first field is symbolic and

corresponds to the SQL command, the second is a binary vector that contains 1 in its i-th position if the i-th relation is projected in the SQL query. The third field is a vector of n vectors, where n is the number of relations in the database. Element `PROJ-ATTR-BIN[i][j]` is equal to 1 if the SQL query projects the j-th attribute of the i-th relation; it is equal to 0 otherwise. Similarly, the fourth field is a binary vector that contains 1 in its i-th position if the i-th relation is used in the SQL query predicate. The fifth field is a vector of n vectors, where n is the number of relations in the database. Element `SEL-ATTR-BIN[i][j]` is equal to 1 if the SQL query references the j-th attribute of the i-th relation in the query predicate; it is equal to 0 otherwise.

It is important to notice that the m-quiplet and the f-quiplet representations use bitmap techniques to encode information about which tables and which columns are used in the query. Notice also that apart from which attributes are used in projection clause and the qualification clause of queries—information encoded by the finest grained representation—no information is provided about the format of the predicates in the qualification clauses. Experiments carried out on experimental data have shown that including the specific format of predicates would not improve the anomaly detection efficiency. Figure 4.2 shows an example query and the three different representations for this query.

The three different representations have been experimentally assessed on a set of SQL traces from a healthcare application and on a synthetic dataset. The experimental results have shown that in general the f-quiplet provides the best performance in terms of accuracy; however, in some cases, also the m-quiplet provides a good representation.

In addition to supporting multiple representations, this syntax-based anomaly detection system supports two classes of subjects: roles, and users. When roles are used, that is, when the DBMS of interest supports RBAC as access control model, the profiles are associated with roles, rather than directly with users. The use of roles has the advantage of reducing the number of required profiles, as typically there are much less roles than users.

When profiles are associated with roles, anomaly detection is based on supervised learning and consists of two phases. The first phase, that is, the training phase, creates a naïve Bayes classifier that has roles as classes. The training phase requires having available a log consisting of non-anomalous queries and the role of each query. The second phase is the actual detection phase; whenever a query is issued, the classifier is used for predicting the role associated with the query. If the predicted role is different from the actual role that has issued the query an anomaly is detected. When no roles are used, the problem of forming user profiles is clearly unsupervised and it is treated as a clustering problem. The specific methodology used is as follows. The training data are partitioned into clusters using standard clustering techniques and a mapping is maintained for every user to its representative cluster. The representative cluster for a user is the cluster that contains the maximum number of training records for that user after the clustering phase. For every new query under observation, its representative cluster is determined by examining the user-cluster mapping. For the detection phase, two approaches have been developed. The first approach applies a naïve Bayes classifier in a manner similar to the supervised case, to determine whether or not the user associated with the

Schema `T1:{a1, b1, c1}`   `T2:{a2, b2, c2} T3:{a3, b3, c3}`
Query   `Select T1.a1, T1.c1, T2.c2 FROM T1, T2, T3`
             `Where T1.a1=T2.a2 AND T1.a1 =T3.a3`

Coarse Quiplet

Field	Value
Command	Select
Num. Projection Tables	2
Num. Projection Columns	3
Num. Selection Tables	3
Num. Selection Columns	3

Medium Quiplet

Field	Value
Command	Select
Projection Tables	[1 1 0]
Projection Columns	[2 1 0]
Selection Tables	[1 1 1]
Selection Columns	[1 1 1]

Fine Quiplet

Field	Value
Command	Select
Projection Tables	[1 1 0]
Projection Columns	[[1 0 1] [0 0 1] [0 0 0]]
Selection Tables	[1 1 1]
Selection Columns	[[1 0 0] [1 0 0] [1 0 0]]

Figure 4.2: An example of different representations of query features.

query belongs to its representative cluster. In the second approach, a statistical test is used to identify if the query is an outlier in its representative cluster. If the result of the statistical test is positive, the query is marked as an anomaly and an alarm is raised.

A main advantage of the syntax-based anomaly detection is that it is a lightweight approach, especially when integrated with the database engine, as in the case of the approach described in this section. The main disadvantage of this approach is that because it does not use any semantic information about queries, it may not be always accurate and in particular may not be able to detect maliciously crafted queries aiming at data harvesting [Mathew et al., 2010]; examples of such queries are queries whose the qualification clause have predicates that are always evaluated to the Boolean value true, like the predicate 'A $\geq$ 10 OR A $<$ 10'.

4.2   DATA-BASED ANOMALY DETECTION

Data-based anomaly detection is based on analyzing the semantics of the query, that is, what the query retrieves, instead of analyzing the query syntax. An approach to characterize what the query retrieves was proposed by Mathew et al. [2010] and consists of collecting for each attribute retrieved by each query a number of statistics. In particular, for numeric attributes the following statistics are collected: min value, max value, mean, median, and standard deviation. Whereas for non-numeric attributes the following statistics are collected: total count of values, and number of distinct values. The statistics collected for all the attributes retrieved by a query are summarized in a query summary vector referred to as *S-Vector*. The profile of a user consists of all the S-Vectors corresponding to the queries issued by this user. With respect to the architecture, this anomaly detection system is located between the applications and the database. It intercepts each query issued to the database and analyzes the query results to determine whether it is anomalous, that is, if the S-Vector of the query does not match the S-Vector of any of the queries in the user profile.

A major problem of this anomaly detection system is that determining whether a query is anomalous requires to fully executing the query, which may not be acceptable for performance. Therefore, approaches based on sampling may have to be adopted by which the statistics are computed on a subset of the query results. However, these sampling approaches may not work correctly if different executions of the same query may return tuples ordered differently, which may be a consequence of different query optimization strategies adopted in different executions of the same query. Also if the query results are computed and returned incrementally to the users or applications, as in the case of cursor-based result retrieval, such a system may not be able to prevent access to the data by malicious queries. However, the principle of characterizing the query results is interesting in order to better profile queries.

4.3   ANOMALY RESPONSE SYSTEMS

The specific handling of an anomaly may depend on many factors. For example [Kamra and Bertino, 2011], if the table which is being accessed contains very sensitive data, a strong response to the anomaly would be to revoke the privileges corresponding to accesses that are flagged as anomalous. However, if the user action is part of a bulk-load operation, when all objects are expected to be accessed by the request, no response action may be necessary. To address the need of different response actions to anomalies, the approach proposed by Kamra and Bertino [2011] uses a response engine which based on information about the anomaly and a response policy base automatically determines the action to execute.

An important component of such response engine is represented by a suitable language for expressing the response engine. The language proposed by Kamra and Bertino [2011] is based on an extension of the well-known trigger languages supported by most commercial DBMSs and widely investigated in past research. Triggers represent a natural mechanism to model response actions. Detection of an anomaly can be seen as an event; moreover, anomalies are characterized by some anomaly attributes again which conditions can be tested. The extension to the conventional trigger format has been introduced to support interactive response actions, which require interactions with the users. An example of an interactive response action is to suspend the access by the user, require the user to perform a stronger authentication, and if the authentication is successful, to allow the access. The format of a response policy is as follows:

```
ON {Event} IF {Condition} THEN {Initial Action}
CONFIRM {Confirmation Action}
ON SUCCESS {Resolution Action}
ON FAILURE {Failure Action} .
```

Conditions are expressed with respect to anomaly attributes categorized into: contextual attributes that include user-id, role-id, sourceIP, date/time, session, client application; and structural attributes that include database name, schema, objects, object attributes, and SQL commands. Possible response actions are categorized into three different classes.

- **Conservative actions.** These have low severity and include actions such as: Nop, which allows the access to be executed; Log, which allows the access but performs a log of the access and related context information; and Alert, which allows the access but sends an alert to some administrator.

- **Fine-grained actions.** These have medium severity and include actions such as: Suspend, which puts the request on hold, until some specific actions may be executed by the user, such as the execution of additional authentication steps; and Taint, which marks a request as potentially suspicious resulting in further monitoring of the user and possibly in the suspension or dropping of subsequent requests by the same user.

- **Aggressive actions.** These have high severity and are typically used to block the access and include actions such as: Abort, which aborts the anomalous request; Disconnect, which disconnect the user session; Revoke, which revoke the user privileges; and Deny, which denies the user privileges.

It is important to notice that a sequence of response actions can also be specified as a response. For example, a Log action can be executed before Alert action in order to log the anomaly details, as well as to send a notification to the security administrator. Also, more complex actions can be devised; for example the user environment may be dynamically isolated so to allow the user to access the data while at the same time preventing the data from being transferred out of the environment, or video surveillance cameras may be automatically switched on.

As an example of the response policy language, the response policy stating "If there is an anomalous write to tables in the 'dbo' schema from un-privileged users inside the organizational internal network, the user should be disconnected" is expressed as follows:

```
ON ANOMALY DETECTION
   IF   Role != DBA                  and
        SourceIP IN 192.168.0.0/16   and
        Obj Type = table             and
        Objs IN dbo.*                and
```

```
                    SQLCmd IN {Insert, Update, Delete}
        THEN DISCONNECT.
```

An example of a more complex policy is the following: "Un-privileged users who are logged from inside the organizational internal network must be re-authenticated for write anomalies to tables in the 'dbo' schema. If the authentication fails, the request has to be dropped and the user disconnected; otherwise no action has to be executed." This policy is expressed as follows:

```
ON ANOMALY DETECTION
        IF Role != DBA              and
        SourceIP IN 192.168.0.0/16  and
        Obj Type = table            and
        Objs IN dbo.*               and
        SQLCmd IN {Insert, Update, Delete}
THEN SUSPEND
CONFIRM re-authenticate
ON SUCCESS NOP
ON FAILURE ABORT, DISCONNECT.
```

An important issue in the implementation is represented by the policy matching, which determines the policy or set of policies matching a given anomaly, and the order according to which the policies must be enforced in the case more in which than one policy matches the anomaly. Two different strategies have been developed for policy matching and both strategies are quite efficient in that even for large number of predicates (120 predicates), the policy matching times are below 0.5ms. With respect to the order to which the matching policies are enforced, two different modes are available among which the DBA can choose:

- **Most Severe Policy (MSP).** The severity level of a response policy is determined by the highest severity level of its response action. This strategy selects the most severe policy from the set of matching policies based on an ordering of the response actions previously described. Also, in the case of interactive response policies, the severity of the policy is taken as the severity level of the Failure Action.

- **Least Severe Policy (LSP).** This strategy selects the least severe policy and as the MSP policy is based on an ordering of the response actions.

We refer the reader to Kamra and Bertino [2011] for a detailed discussion of experimental results and implementation details.

4.4   RESEARCH DIRECTIONS

The design and development of anomaly detection systems for databases is an important research direction which to date has not been much investigated. There are many open research directions. One important direction is represented by the definition and implementation of richer feature vectors for representing queries. One interesting approach is to extend the approach by Kamra et al. [2008], described in Section 4.1, with the addition of the selectivity estimations for queries. The estimations can be obtained from the query optimizer. The advantage of this approach, compared with the data-based anomaly detection described in Section 4.2, is that it does not require executing the query and therefore the query can be analyzed for anomalies before its execution. A related direction is represented by a more comprehensive representation of the insider behavior that could include information such as the context of the access (location, time, IP address, and so on), the query sequences, accesses to data catalogues, duration of the sessions, and so forth. Another important direction is related to the profile evolution over time. Anomaly detection systems usually have an initial phase in which the profiles of the normal behaviors are created. However, the behaviors of users may change over time and therefore the profiles have to be updated accordingly without undermining data access continuity.

Finally, it is important to emphasize that in addition to control the accesses performed by the insiders in order to detect anomalous queries, it is crucial to detect how the data are used after having been accessed. In many attacks, stolen data may be moved to other machines (for example development machines) before being transmitted outside the organization [Bertino and Ghinita, 2011a]. Therefore, it is crucial to construct *data flow profiles* able to characterize the flow of the data both inside and outside the organization, and then use these profiles to detect anomalous data movements. To date there are no approaches able to characterize data flows and to detect anomalies. However, recent techniques for modeling and capturing provenance [Sultana and Bertino, 2012] can be used to create and use these profiles for data flow anomaly detection.

CHAPTER 5

Security Information and Event Management and Auditing

Security information and event management (SIEM) refers to tools and processes for the centralized real-time collection, integration, and analysis of logs and events occurring in a distributed system. The main advantage of the use of centralized SIEM tools is that they not only provide unified interfaces to a variety of disparate data, but they also allow one to correlate, in real-time, different events occurring in different parts of the system and therefore to early detect threats to the system. As SIEM tools collect a large amount of information about user activities, data accesses, and application and incident management, they are crucial not only for security, but also for compliance reporting and auditing, and threat management. Also, as these tools provide long-term storage of the collected security and event information, they can be used for forensics, that is, when investigating security incidents, and also for enhancing the security posture of organizations. In the context of protection from insider threats, SIEM tools can be very helpful in supporting the creation of comprehensive profiles of insider activities that can be used for detecting anomalies, as discussed in Chapter 4 of the lecture.

Because of their relevance for security and compliance, SIEM tools have been widely developed by industry and a large number of products exist today on the market as well as well open source tools[1](OSS). We refer the reader to a recent Gartner report [Nicolett and Kavanagh, 2011] for detailed comparison of 25 commercial products.

A major issue in general with SIEM tools is that as they were initially designed as tools for networks, their integration with applications can be challenging especially when applications have not been designed to include specific functions for application-level logging. Also, these tools are not able to support fine-grained audit on data stored in a database, even though some of them have support for file integrity monitoring. Fine-grained auditing refers to determining which specific data records (e.g., tuples) were actually disclosed while processing a given query [Agrawal et al., 2004]. Fine-grained auditing is crucial for investigation of data security breaches by insiders.

In what follows, we first outline the main components of a SIEM tool (Section 5.1). We then overview approaches in the area of fine-grained auditing for database systems (Section 5.2), and discuss open research directions (Section 5.3).

---

[1]Open Source SIEM: http://communities.alienvault.com/community

5.1   COMPONENTS OF A SIEM TOOL

A SIEM tool usually consists of two main components: (a) the Security Information Management (SIM) component that is in charge of collecting and logging all security-relevant information and supporting compliance; and (b) the Security Event Management (SEM) component that is in charge of intrusion detection, event correlation, and incident response. In the past, these two components usually corresponded to different tools and products; today, however, they are usually integrated into a single comprehensive tool.

Input to the SIM components is from multiple sources, including intrusion detection systems, syslog tools, firewall logs, vulnerability scan tools, log export application tools, and may require the deployment of sensor agents in charge of capturing security relevant information. As those sources may encode security-relevant information in different formats, a draft standard had been proposed in order to facilitate integration of this information[2], which, however, is still under development. The data collected from the various agents are then stored into a log which is typically highly secured through encryption. The deployment of sensor agents is typically a critical issue in the deployment of a SIEM tools, as these agents may slow down performance and my in turn introduce vulnerabilities.

The SEM is in charge of using the integrated collected data for a number of different functions, including event correlation, vulnerability scanning, data mining for events, real-time monitoring, and data assets tracking. In particular, it is important to notice that event correlation is much more powerful than event aggregation. An example of event correlation is detecting that large number of messages sent by different nodes in a large distributed system are all directed towards the same destination node, which may be indicative of a distributed denial attack being launched by this system [Lee et al., 2011]. The SEM component typically has sophisticated reporting capabilities as different administrators and managers of the system may be interested in different statistics and data or may need different reports for different compliance requirements.

5.2   FINE-GRAINED AUDITING

Fine-grained auditing has been specifically investigated in the context of privacy-preserving database systems [Agrawal et al., 2004] with the goal of detecting when specific tuples are accessed. Notice that SIEM tools are often able to collect information about queries being issued by users in the monitored system. However, they typically only record the SQL statements that have been issued and not the query results. Thus, because data change overtime, re-running such queries may not always allow one to identify the actual tuples that had been accessed when the queries had been originally issued. Also it is not trivial to specify exactly when a tuple has been used by a query, as it may have been used to produce the results, for example used for computing the results of a subquery, but not actually returned to the users.

---

[2]OpenXDAS: http://openxdas.sourceforge.net/

The first approach to fine-grained auditing for databases has been proposed by Agrawal et al. [2004] with the goal of supporting query auditing in case of data privacy breaches. Their approach is based on three main components.

- A backlog database storing all queries ran against the database. The logged queries are annotated with the identifier of the user that ran the query, the time of the query, and the query's purpose. The backlog database also stores all updates to the base tables in some backlog table to be able to recover the actual database state at the time when each logged query was ran. Capturing the updates is based on the use of query triggers. Because temporal information is crucial in order to reconstruct the correct database state with respect to a given past query, two different organizations were proposed to represent temporal information, namely: a time stamped organization, and an interval stamped organization.

- An SQL statement to specify audit expressions. Such a statement specifies a set of data with respect to which an audit has to be performed, that is, it determines which queries have accessed this data. Audit expressions allow one to specify at a fine-grained level of precision the data to be audited; thus one may even specify a single column within a single tuple. More specifically the syntax of an audit expression is as follows:

```
[during start-time to end-time]
audit audit-list
from table-list
where condition-list
```

The during clause allows one to require searching for queries that accessed the data in a certain time interval. The other clauses specify, respectively: the data of interest to the audit, specified as column names; the tables storing this data; and the tuples storing this data within these tables.

An example of audit expression specified against tables Customer and Treatment is the following [Agrawal et al., 2004]:

```
audit disease
from Customer c, Treatment t
where c.cid = t.pcid and c.zip = '95120';
```

Such audit expression specifies that the data of interest to the audit are the data about the diseases of patients living at addresses with zip code equal to 95120.

- An approach to generate auditing queries and to identify suspicious queries. As not all queries may be relevant to a given audit expression, a first step in the audit process consists of identifying through a static analysis the queries that are non-candidates for the auditing. Such queries typically include the queries that were executed in time intervals different from the time interval associated with the audit expression, or queries that accessed columns other than the columns specified in the audit expression, or queries whose predicates are in contradiction with the predicates in the `where` clause of the audit expression. Once the non-candidate queries have been eliminated, the remaining queries, referred to as potentially suspicious queries with respect to the audit expressions, are each combined with the audit expression, resulting in a set of auditing queries. Each auditing query is then run against a database reconstructed from the backlog database so to be identical to the actual database at the time when the original query was run. If the result of the execution of the audit query is non-empty, the query is determined to be suspicious with respect to the audit expression. The notion of suspicious query is also formally defined in the paper by Agrawal et al. [2004] and is based on the concept of indispensable tuple with respect to a query Q, that is, a tuple that if missing will result in a different result for Q. A query is suspicious with respect to an audit query, if the query and the audit expression share at least an indispensable tuple. These notions have been formally defined and explored in [Agrawal et al., 2004].

A later paper by Kaushik and Ramamurthy [2011] explored the problem of data auditing following the same ideas of the earlier work by Agrawal et al. and resulted in some minor theoretical extensions.

5.3   RESEARCH DIRECTIONS

Logging and auditing are important functions for protection against insider threats and also for investigation of data security breaches. Tools for logging, correlating, and analyzing security information and events have been developed by many different companies. These tools have mainly originated from techniques developed for networks and therefore they do not support fine-grained auditing capabilities for data accesses. Research in the database area has proposed some initial approaches to fine-grained data auditing. However, these approaches do not address the problem of what happens to the data after have been accessed, in that they are limited to determining whether a query may have accessed certain data items. One would need, however, to track the use of the accessed data items as these data items could be copied into other data items that could then be misused. In this respect, data lineage techniques could help tracing the derivation of data sets from other data sets and thus improving data misuse detection. Another specific research question is whether temporal DBMS could be used for query auditing.

CHAPTER 6

Separation of Duty

Separation of duty (SoD) is a key principle in computer security. In 1975, Saltzer and Schroder [1975] identified SoD as one of the eight design principles for the protection of information in computer systems. As discussed by Simon and Zurko [1997]: *"Separation of Duty is a security principle used to formulate multi-person control policies, requiring that two or more different people be responsible for the completion of a task or set of related tasks. The purpose of this principle is to discourage fraud by spreading the responsibility and authority for an action or task over multiple people, thereby raising the risk involved in committing a fraudulent act by requiring the involvement of more than one individual."* A frequently used example refers to the tasks of preparing a purchase order and approving the order. A SoD policy for these tasks would require that the subject preparing the order be different from the subject approving the order. If different individuals are required for creating and approving orders, then committing fraud requires a conspiracy of at least two, which raises the risk of fraud detection significantly.

SoD is crucial for protection from malicious insiders as insiders typically act alone when performing malicious actions and therefore techniques that would mandate the collaboration of several insiders to perform a sensitive activity would require the malicious insider to collude with other insiders, thus making the attack more difficult to perpetrate. However, despite its importance as a security principle, very few approaches have been proposed to support SoD in computer systems. The main reason, as discussed by Gligor et al. [1998], is that SoD is an inherently application-oriented policy and, therefore, it is very difficult to provide support for it at lower levels within computer systems. In particular, the definition of SoD policy requires the identification of well-defined application tasks corresponding to security-critical actions. However, a few pioneering approaches have been proposed that show approaches to enforce SoD policies in different contexts that we discuss in this chapter.

We start by a presentation of a SoD model and enforcement engine proposed by Bertino et al. [1999a] for workflow systems, widely known as the BFA model (Section 6.1). As workflows organize business processes and applications in terms of tasks and dependencies among tasks, they represent a natural setting in which to apply SoD policies. We then present an approach by which SoD is directly supported by a DBMS [Kamra and Bertino, 2011] (Section 6.2); SoD is used here to require that certain security sensitive operations, namely management of security policies, must be authorized jointly by several DBAs. Even though the application is limited only to policy management, it represents an interesting application of SoD that could be further extended to other security critical administrative operations. We then present an application of SoD recently proposed in the context of location-based access control (Section 6.3); here, the SoD policy requires that the presence of several individuals in order to allow one individual to perform a specific action [Kirkpatrick et al., 2011]. We finally conclude the chapter by outlining open research directions.

6.1   SOD FOR WORKFLOW SYSTEMS—THE BFA MODEL

In the BFA model a workflow consists of multiple tasks, each of which is executed by a subject according to the execution authorizations specified for the workflow. The execution authorization model is based on the Hierarchical RBAC model (cf. Chapter 3) in that the permissions to execute the workflow tasks are typically granted to roles that are organized into role hierarchies. The BFA model complements this RBAC execution authorization model by supporting the specification of a large variety of SoD constraints. An important classification of these constraints is into *static SoD constraints*, and *dynamic SoD constraints*. Static SoD constraints are based on specifying different roles for different tasks in the workflow. Whereas dynamic SoD constraints specify that even though the same role can execute two different tasks, different individuals, under the same role, must execute these tasks. Therefore, the enforcement of dynamic SoD constraints requires a dynamic enforcement at run-time based on the actual usage of roles by users. Static SoD constraints can be evaluated without executing the workflow, whereas the dynamic SoD constraints can only be evaluated at during the execution of the workflow, because they express restrictions based on the execution history of the workflow. The BFA model includes a third category of constraints, referred to as *hybrid SoD constraints*; the satisfiability of these constraints can be partially verified without executing the workflow.

The following example illustrates the discussion. Consider a simple activity dealing with a tax refund, which can be modeled by a workflow consisting of four tasks to be executed sequentially (see Figure 6.1):

- Task T_1: A clerk prepares a check for a tax refund.

- Task T_2: A manager can approve or disapprove the check. This task should be performed twice by two different managers. The check will be issued if both the managers approve it; it will be voided otherwise.

- Task T_3: The decisions of the managers are collected and the final decision is made. The manager who collects the results must be different from those executing task T_2.

- Task T_4: A clerk issues or voids the check based on the result of task T_3; the clerk issuing or voiding the check must be different from the clerk who prepared the check.

In the above example, each task is assigned a role, namely, T_1 and T_4 must be executed by a role "clerk," whereas T_2 and T_3 must be executed by a role "manager." So the various duties, and the corresponding authorizations, are statically separated by imposing the rule that different roles execute different tasks. An example of dynamic separation of duties is the constraint that a particular clerk must not execute both tasks T_1 and T_4 for the same check. However, he or she can perform task T_1

on some checks, while performing task T_4 for other checks. Therefore, a clerk cannot issue or void a check he or she prepared.

It is important to emphasize that if there is no proper support, constraints such as separation of duties must be implemented as application code and embedded into the various tasks. Such an approach makes the specification and management of authorization constraints difficult if not impossible, given the large number of tasks that typically occur in a workflow.

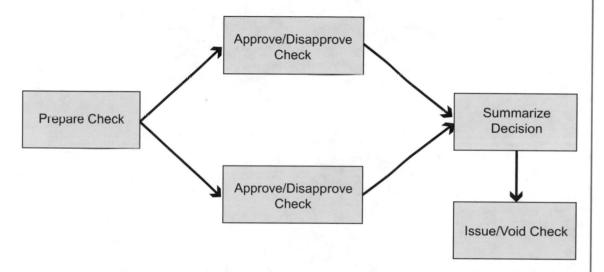

Figure 6.1: A (simplified) workflow representing a tax refund process.

As mentioned, roles are organized according to a role hierarchy defined based on a global partial order, denoted by >, on the role set. Such an order usually reflects the organizational position of roles within an organization. Let R_i, R_j be roles. We say that R_i dominates R_j if $R_i > R_j$. Figure 6.2 illustrates an example of role order, where there is an arc from role R_i to role R_j if $R_i > R_j$. We assume by default that if R_i dominates R_j, then R_j should be given higher priority over R_i when assigning a role to the task. However, if no authorized user is available to play role R_j and execute the task, then the task can be executed by any user playing role R_i. As an example, consider the roles in Figure 6.2 and suppose that role Refund Clerk is associated with task T_1 of our tax refund processing example. This means that, by default, the task of preparing a check is assigned to the Refund Clerk. However, if no user authorized to play role Refund Clerk is available to execute the task, then the task can be executed by any user playing role Refund Manager or General Manager, since both Refund Manager and General Manager precede Refund Clerk in the role order.

Moreover, it is possible to locally (at the task level) refining the role global order. For each task of the workflow, the global order can be refined by specifying additional *local* order relationships for roles where there is no relationship in the global order.

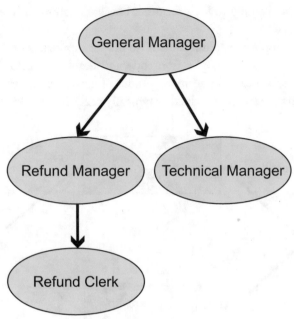

Figure 6.2: An example of role hierarchy.

As mentioned earlier, the BFA model supports the specification of many different constraints, for which a formal model has been developed based on normal logic programs [Lloyd, 1984]. The BFA model also supports the specification of *binding of duty* (BoD) constraints, which require that certain tasks be executed by the same users. Even BoD constraints have not been investigated or applied, they may be useful for enforcing the execution of obligations by users upon data accesses or task execution. As such, they can have a critical role for insider threat protection.

The following are examples of constraints that can be expressed in the BFA model. The constraints refer to the workflow introduced earlier, shown in Figure 6.1, and the role hierarchy shown in Figure 6.2.

- **C1:** At least three roles must be associated with the workflow.

- **C2:** Task T_2 must be executed by a role dominating the roles that execute tasks T_1 and T_4, unless T_1, T_2, and T_4 are executed by the role General Manager.

- **C3:** If a user who belongs to role Refund Clerk and has performed task T_1, then he/she cannot perform T_4.

- **C4:** If a user has performed task T_2, then he/she cannot perform task T_3.

- **C5:** Each activation of task T_2 within the same workflow must be executed by a different user.

- **C6:** If more than four activations of task T_1, within the same workflow, executed by one single individual abort, then the same person cannot execute task T_1 anymore. Here abort refers to the abnormal completion of the task due to user errors, or system or application errors.

- **C7:** If Bob executes task T_2, then he cannot execute task T_4.

Constraint C1 is a static constraint since the number of roles associated with the workflow can be checked by simply considering the workflow role specification. Constraints C2, C3, C4, C5, and C7 are hybrid constraints. Preliminary consistency verification can be performed for these constraints without executing the workflow. If they are found to be inconsistent, they will certainly not be satisfied by the workflow execution. For instance, if a single user is associated with task T_2, constraint C5 will never be satisfied during workflow execution. If, however, the above condition is not verified, it is necessary to check during workflow execution that whenever a user executes an activation of task T_2, the same user does not execute any further activation of task T_2. Similarly, constraint C2 will never be satisfied at execution time if each role associated with task T_2 is dominated by the least upper bound of the set of roles associated with T_1 or T_4. Finally, constraint C6 is dynamic, since no check on its consistency can be performed without executing the workflow.

A formal definition of consistency for the constraint language of the BFA model has been developed based on a formal semantics of the constraint language. The semantics is based on the *stable model semantics* of logic programs with negation [Gelfond and Lifschitz, 1988]. Based on this formal model, a role planner has also been designed which is in charge of assigning one or more roles for execution to each task in a workflow by assuring that the maximum number of constraints are satisfied. Note that such role planning is quite complex, and may have to execute multiple times during the execution of the workflow. We refer the reader to Bertino et al. [1999a] for the details about the formal semantics and the planning algorithms.

6.2   THE JOINT THRESHOLD ADMINISTRATION MODEL

The joint threshold administration model (JTAM) was proposed by Kamra and Bertino [2011] in the context of an anomaly detection system (see Chapter 4). The goal of this administration model is to prevent DBA from deactivating or modifying anomaly response policies, which determine how anomalies are managed. For example, if one such policy specifies that upon access to some user data by a DBA, an alarm has to be triggered, a malicious DBA may simply deactivate the policy before performing the access and re-activate the policy right after.

JTAM is the first model that applies the SoD principle to security administration. It controls the administration actions concerning those policies by requiring that multiple DBA authorize each administration action concerning the policies. The actual mechanism used for implementing this form of SoD is based on the use of threshold cryptography signatures [Shoup, 2000]. The basic paradigm of most well-known threshold signature schemes is as follows [Gennaro et al., 2007]. Each user U_i has a share s_i (that is, a portion) of the secret key corresponding to the signature key d. Each user U_i participating in the signature generation protocol generates a signature share that takes as input the message m (or the hash of the message) that needs to be signed, the secret key share s_i, and other public information. Signature shares from different users are then combined to form the final valid signature on m. A DBA thus authorizes a policy operation, such as create or drop a policy, by submitting a signature share on the policy. At least k signature shares are required to form a valid final signature on a policy, where k is a threshold parameter defined for each policy at the time of policy creation. The final signature is then validated either periodically or upon policy usage to detect any malicious modifications to the policies.

The various steps and functions of JTAM are based on the policy lifecycle (see Figure 6.3). Initially, a policy is created by a DBA; as part of the policy creation command, the number k of DBA that have to authorize administrative actions on the newly created policy is also specified. Once the policy has been created, it must be authorized for activation by at least k-1 DBA after which the DBMS changes the state of the policy to ACTIVATED. Each DBA submits his/her authorization by submitting his/her own signature share.

To alter/drop a policy or to make it non-operational, the policy state must be changed to SUS-PENDED. To change the policy state to SUSPENDED, a DBA issues the `Suspend Response Policy` command. This command has the effect of initially changing the state of the policy into the SUSPEND IN-PROGRESS state indicating that additional authorizations for the policy suspension are being collected; while in this state the policy remains operational. Once all the k authorizations have been collected, the policy state changes to SUSPEND. Similar steps are followed for other administrative actions, including `DROP`, and for changes to the policy.

JTAM has several advantages. First, it requires no changes to the existing access control mechanisms of a DBMS for achieving SoD. Second, the final signature on a policy is non-repudiable, thus making the DBA accountable for authorizing a policy operation. Third, and probably the most important, JTAM allows an organization to utilize existing man-power resources to address the problem of insider threats since it is no longer required to employ additional users as policy administrators. It is, however, important to observe that a collaborative administration model, like JTAM, has to deal with administrative actions whose execution may take a non-negligible amount of time due to the asynchronous execution of authorization steps by the different DBA involved, which may not be always acceptable.

6.3   PROXIMITY LOCATION CONSTRAINTS

Existing location-based access control models have the major shortcoming of focusing only on the location of the user issuing the access request. However, in many real situations whether a user can access some resources may depend on the presence or absence of other users. As an example, consider a government agency with data classified at multiple levels of security. One policy could prohibit access to a sensitive document if there are any civilians (i.e., non-governmental employees) present. Another could require the presence of a supervisor when a document is signed. Yet another could require that the subject is alone (e.g., "for your eyes only" restrictions). In particular, constraints that require the presence of multiple users may be used for enforcing a SoD policy.

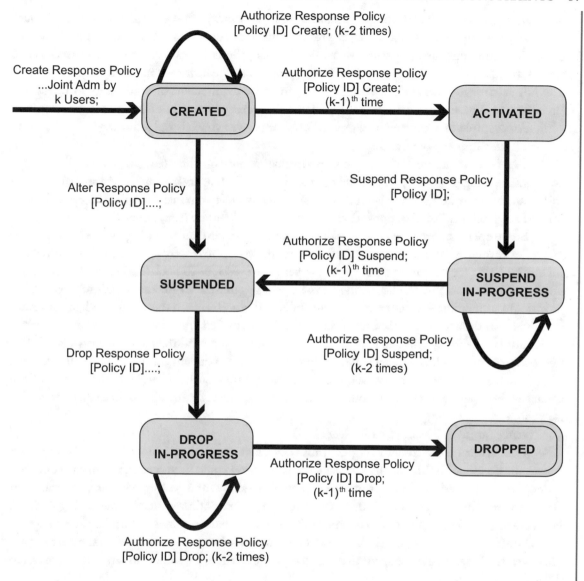

Figure 6.3: Policy state transition diagram [Kamra and Bertino, 2011].

A constraint model supporting the above notions was recently proposed by Kirkpatrick et al. [2011] for the RBAC access control model. This constraint model, referred to as *prox-RBAC*, is based on the key notion of *proximity constraint*, that is, is a security requirement that is satisfied by the location of other users. If the constraint must be continuously evaluated for the duration of the user's access session, then the constraint is *continuous*. Proximity constraints are built from three primitive constructs: relative constraint clauses, continuity of usage constraints, and timeouts. *Relative constraint clauses* define the static presence or absence conditions that must be met. However, mobile environments are inherently dynamic. As such, the latter two constructs are necessary to ensure the relative constraint clause is enforced properly as the environment changes.

A *relative constraint clause* specifies the proximity requirement of other users in the spatial environment. These clauses can be described as either presence constraints or absence constraints.

An example of a constraint, expressed by an intuitive syntax, is the following:

at_least2 supervisors in Room 105

The basic structure consists of an optional cardinality qualifier (e.g., *at_least* or *at_most*), a nonnegative integer specifying the number of subjects, a role (e.g., *supervisor*), and a spatial relationship (e.g., *in Room 105*). The spatial relationship consists of two parts: a topological relation (e.g., *in*) and a logical location descriptor that identifies a spatial feature (e.g., *Room 105*).

Some operations may require a significant duration. For instance, reading a sensitive document may take several minutes or hours. Furthermore, it may be necessary to ensure that the relative constraint holds for the entire duration of the permitted session. To declare whether the constraint must be checked only at the beginning of the session or must hold for the duration, prox-RBAC provides two qualifiers for continuity of usage, called *when* and *while*, respectively. A when constraint is evaluated at the access request time; if the constraint is satisfied, the permission is granted. A while constraint is repeatedly checked and the permission is granted until the constraint is violated. The frequency of the check is a system-wide parameter that is dependent on the deployment scenario. That is, specifying this parameter requires considering issues such as network latency, size of the spatial environment, number and mobility of users. An example of constraint using the *while* qualifier is as follows:

while (at_least 2 supervisors in Room 105)

One critical issue in enforcing continuity of usage constraints is how to react once a *while* constraint no longer holds. In one scenario, the permission could be suspended until the condition is once again satisfied. In others, it may be acceptable to allow some leeway, wherein the permission is still granted for a short duration of time, even though the condition is technically being violated. For instance, consider a proximity constraint that specifies that a supervisor must be present to read an accounting record. Due to a shift change, one supervisor leaves the room before the next arrives. However, the break is short enough that it is acceptable to allow the subject to retain the permission during their absences.

A language like prox-RBAC can represent an effective mechanism for SoD. The notion of proximity that in prox-RBAC is based on the physical presence of other individuals in the same space can be extended to cyberspace, for example by requiring that a user doing a security critical action must share his/her screen with other users. Scenarios like this one are today possible due to the large number of tools supporting collaborative activities of remotely located users and innovations in the area of tele-presence.

6.4   RESEARCH DIRECTIONS

Tools and techniques to enforce SoD policies can represent effective mechanisms for protection against malicious insiders. The design and implementation of SoD tools and techniques tailored to databases and their applications remains a major open research direction; except for the approaches described in Sections 6.1 and 6.2, there are no other approaches. An interesting research issue is to investigate how the joint threshold administration model, described in Section 6.2, can be adopted for other security-sensitive administrative operations, such as the GRANT operation for issuing authorizations to users, or to data accesses operations—for example, one may require that accesses to some user data by a DBA to user data much be jointly approved by other DBA/security officers. Support for SoD at authorization level is also important and would allow one to specify that certain authorizations are mutually exclusive, that is, they cannot be used during the same session. For example, the usage of an authorization to access certain sensitive data would be mutually exclusive with the authorization to send e-mail or to write into other data, while the data are being accessed.

CHAPTER 7

Case Study—Oracle Database Vault

Commercial DBMSs today provide various tools to ensure data security and privacy, ranging from fine-grained access control to multilevel security [Oracle, 2006], and cell-level and full-database encryption [Microsoft, 2008] and thus can help protecting against insider threats. One interesting tool aimed at specifically protecting data from insiders with system privileges (including DBA) is represented by Oracle Database Vault [Oracle, 2012a]. Protection against these insiders is quite challenging as these insiders have typically a lot of privileges and are also technically skilled users. In what follows, we present an overview of the main components of Oracle Vault and we refer the reader to Bertino et al. [2011] for details about fine-grained access control in commercial DBMS.

Oracle Database Vault had been developed with the goal of addressing regulatory compliance requirements. These requirements arise in a number of different laws and regulations, such as HIPAA, and Serbanes-Oaxley in the U.S., and typically mandate that data be protected from un-authorized accesses and/or un-authorized accesses from all users of a database, including DBA and other users with high privileges. In order to achieve stronger protection Oracle Database Vault supports the partitioning of a database into different *realms* and provides four different security techniques (see Figure 7.1 from Oracle [2007]): rule sets and command rules, multi-factor authorization, separation of duty, and reports. In what follows we discuss in more details some of these components.

7.1 REALMS

The notion of realm is a first important component of Oracle Data Vault. It allows one to partition a database into multiple partitions and segregate different partitions from different users with system privileges. A realm is a functional grouping of database schema, objects, and roles that must be secured and support the enforcement of fine-grained access control for users that have system privileges like "create any table" and "delete any table." For example, in an organization with different functional sectors (finance, human resources), one could define a realm for each such sector, like:

- the set of schemas, objects, and roles that are related to finance; and

- the set of schemas, objects, and roles that are related to human resources.

The possibility of including roles (of the RBAC model) into a realm for protection is particularly important in that it prevents insiders with system privileges from being able to use roles that they should not be using according to the organizational policies.

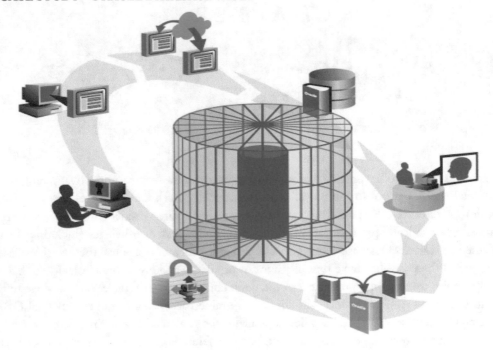

Figure 7.1: Main concepts of Oracle Vault [Oracle, 2007].

Realm management is supported by a number of procedures (part of the Oracle `DVSYS.DBMS_MACADM` package), including procedures for creating realms, registering a set of scheme objects or roles (secured objects) for realm protection, granting authorizations on realms, and running reports on realms.

A realm is created by invoking the `CREATE_REALM` procedure (see Figure 7.2 for the procedure interface definition and an example). Notice the audit options specified through the parameter `audit_options` that allows one to select one among the following four audit capabilities.

- *Audit Disabled* (0): It does not create an audit record.

- *Audit On Failure* (1): It is the default option and creates an audit record when a realm violation occurs (for example, when an unauthorized user tries to modify an object that is protected by the realm).

- *Audit On Success* (2): It creates an audit record for any authorized activity executed on the realm.

- *Audit On Success or Failure* (3): It creates an audit record for any activity that occurs in the realm, including both authorized and unauthorized activities.

Objects can be dynamically assigned to realms by using the procedure `ADD_OBJECT_TO_REALM`, which simply requires specifying as input the realm name and owner, and the object name and owner. Objects from different schemas or accounts can be under the same realm, and an object can belong to multiple realms.

```
DVSYS.DBMS_MACADM.CREATE_REALM(
        realm_name IN VARCHAR2,
        description IN VARCHAR2,
        enabled IN VARCHAR2,
        audit_options IN NUMBER);
BEGIN
     DVSYS.DBMS_MACADM.CREATE_REALM(
        realm_name => 'Human Resource Realm',
        description => 'Realm to manage HR',
        enabled => DBMS_MACUTL.G_YES,
        audit_options => 3);
     END;
```

Figure 7.2: Definition of the procedure for creating realms and an example of its invocation.

Of course realms, as any other database objects, are protected objects and therefore have their own authorizations. More specifically, a realm authorization establishes when an account or role is authorized to use its system privileges in the following situations:

- when creating, manipulating or accessing realm-secured objects; and

- when granting or revoking realm-secured roles.

A user can be granted realm authorizations as either a *realm owner* or a *realm participant*. These authorizations can only be granted by the `DV_OWNER` and `DV_ADMIN` which are special purpose roles introduced specifically for Oracle Database Vault. A user who has been granted the participant authorization on a realm can only create, manipulate and access the objects protected by the realm. A user who has been granted an owner authorization has the same privileges as a realm participant and can in addition grant and revoke authorizations to roles protected by the realm.

7.2   RULE SETS

Rule sets represent a second important security component as they allow one to further restrict realm authorizations by associating conditions with these authorizations. In other words, these rule sets define when realm authorizations became active. A rule set is typically expressed as a set of conditions (e.g., rules), where each condition is a PL/SQL expression that evaluates to true or false. A rule is created by invoking the `CREATE_RULE` procedure (see Figure 7.3 for an example invocation of this procedure).

```
BEGIN
      DVSYS.DBMS_MACADM.CREATE_RULE(
      rule_name => 'Check UPDATE operations',
      rule_expr=>'SYS_CONTEXT(''USERENV'',''SESSION_USER'')=
      ''SYSADM''');
      END;
```

Figure 7.3: An example of rule creation.

A rule set evaluates to true or false based on the evaluation of each rule it contains and the evaluation type (*All True* or *Any True*). When the *All True* evaluation type is used, all rules in the rule set must evaluate to true for the rule set to evaluate to true, whereas when the *Any True* evaluation type is used, it is sufficient that one rule is evaluated to true for the rule set to evaluate to true. Rule sets can only be created by users who have the DV_OWNER and DV_ADMIN roles by invoking the CREATE_RULE_SET procedure. Other procedures allow one to add and remove rules from rule sets as well as to modify rules and rename rule sets.

7.3   COMMAND RULES

A command rule is a rule created to protect SELECT, ALTER SYSTEM, database definition language (DDL), and data manipulation language (DML) statements that affect one or more database objects. A command rule is essentially a rule set associated with a specific statement. Command rules are enforced at run-time and affect any user who tries to use the SQL statements it protects, regardless of the realm in which the object exists. For example, one can configure a command rule that allows DDL statements such as CREATE TABLE, DROP TABLE, and ALTER TABLE in a given schema to be authorized after business hours, but not during business hours. A command rule consists of the following components.

- The SQL statement protected by the command rule.

- The owner of the object the command rule affects.

- The database object the command rule affects.

- Whether the command rule is enabled.

- A rule set.

Command rules can be categorized into the following.

- **Command rules that have a system-wide scope.** With this type, one can only create one command rule for each database instance. Examples are command rules for the ALTER SYSTEM and CONNECT statements.

- **Command rules that are schema specific.** An example is a command rule for the DROP TABLE statement.

- **Command rules that are object specific.** An example is a command rule for the SELECT statement with a specific table included in the command rule definition.

When a user issues a statement protected by a command rule in a realm, the following steps are executed by Oracle Database Vault.

1. The realm authorization is checked first.

2. If there are no realm violation and if the associated command rules are enabled, the associated rule sets are evaluated.

3. If all the rule sets evaluate to the Boolean value True, then the statement is authorized for further processing.

4. If any of the rule sets evaluates to Boolean value False, then the statement is not authorized and a command rule violation is created.

Notice thus that users with system privileges not only can be restricted to specific realms, but also when allowed to access and manipulate objects in a realm, the actions they execute can be allowed only in very restricted and controlled situations.

7.4   MULTI-FACTOR AUTHORIZATION

The main idea of multi-factor authorization is that applications can configure their own filters, called *factors*, for allowing or denying access to sensitive data. For example, one may only allow access to certain data from a specific IP address or subnet. A factor is essentially a named variable or attribute, such a user location, database IP address, user session, that can used in rule sets and command rules. Oracle provides a large number of predefined factors and also allows the applications to define their own factors.

7.5   SEPARATION OF DUTY

Oracle Database Vault provides some simple form of separation of duty by partitioning the system administrative responsibilities into the following categories and assigning them to different roles.

- **Account management.** Account management entails creating, modifying, and dropping user accounts. The DV_ACCTMGR role provides these privileges.

- **Security administration.** Security administration covers basic security tasks such as creating realms and command rules, setting security policies for database users' access, and authorizing database users for jobs they are allowed to perform. Security administrators also run security audit reports. The DV_OWNER and DV_ADMIN roles provide these privileges.

- **Resource management.** Resource management refers to managing the database system but not accessing business data. It includes the following operations.

  - **Backup operations** require a predefined time to perform the backup using predefined tools.

  - **Tuning and monitoring operations** require ongoing performance monitoring and analysis.

  - **Patching operations** require temporary access only during the time the patching takes place.

7.6   CONCLUDING REMARKS

In this chapter, an overview of the main features of Oracle Database Vault, a comprehensive system for protection against insider threats is presented. Database Vault provides several predefined mechanisms, such as predefined factors, and also allows the applications to define their own mechanisms, for example by implementing application-specific factors. An interesting research/architectural issue is how one could integrate Oracle Database Vault with anomaly detection mechanisms, like the ones discussed in Chapter 4, and application-dependent separation of duty policies.

CHAPTER 8

Conclusion

This lecture has presented an overview of different security techniques that need to be combined to achieve comprehensive solutions against the problem of insider threats. The techniques discussed in the lecture include flexible continuous authentication, fine-grained context based access control, anomaly detection, logging and auditing, and separation of duty policies. Many of these techniques had been proposed with general security goals in mind; however, the discussion throughout the chapters in the lecture points to the specific uses of these techniques for protection from insider threats. The various chapters also point out various open research directions. In addition to these, it is important to mention some additional major research issues.

The first issue concerns how to assure strong protection from insider threats by, at the same time, assuring the privacy of individuals involved for various purposes and functions with the protected data. Tools like anomaly detection and fine-grained access control may require collecting and analyzing a lot of data about the activities and personal habits of such individuals, even including their activities on social networks. This poses a lot of privacy problems. It is thus important to make sure that data collected by monitoring the individuals within an organization be carefully protected and not misused. Also, anomaly detection approaches that could work on encrypted data would be crucial.

The second issue concerns how to protect against data deception attacks by malicious insiders. Data deception refers to a malicious insider planting misleading data into a database. Like data leakage and misuse, data deception attacks also may have severe consequences on organizations. Many techniques discussed in this lecture directly apply to the problem of protection from data deception. However, one also needs techniques to assess whether the data are truthful. Work done in the area of data quality is very relevant here [Batini and Scannapieco, 2006], even though techniques in data quality have not been designed to deal with adversarial environments, as well as recent work in the area of data trustworthiness [Lim et al., 2012].

Finally, it is emphasized that protection from insider threats requires that software be secure and free of vulnerability and that systems be correctly configured. As such, most of the work done in computer and communication system security is very relevant here.

Bibliography

R. Agrawal, R. Bayardo, C. Faloutsos, J. Kiernan, R. Rantzau and R. Srikant (2004) Auditing compliance with a hippocratic database. In *Proc. 30th Int. Conf. on Very Large Data Bases*, pages 516–527. Cited on page(s) 47, 48, 49, 50

D. Agrawal, J. Giles, K. Lee and J. Lobo (2005) Policy ratification. In *Proc. IEEE Int. Workshop on Policies for Distributed Systems and Networks*, pages 223–232. DOI: 10.1109/POLICY.2005.25 Cited on page(s) 34

ANSI (2004) ANSI/INSITS 359–2004 for role based access control. Cited on page(s) 21, 22

M. Astrahan, M. Blasgen, D. Chamberlin, K.P. Eswarean, J. Gray, P.P. Griffith, W.F. King III, R.A. Lorie, P.R. McJones, J.W. Mehl, G.R. Putzolu, I.L. Traiger, B.W. Wade and V. Watson (1976) System R: Relational approach to database management. *ACM Trans. Database Syst.* 1(2), pages 97–137. DOI: 10.1145/320455.320457 Cited on page(s) 19

C. Batini and M. Scannapieco (2006) *Data Quality: Concepts, Methodologies and Techniques*, Springer. Cited on page(s) 67

D. Bell and L. LaPadula (1976) Secure Computer Systems: Unified Exposition and Multics Interpretation. Technical report, MTR-2997, Mitre Corporation. Cited on page(s) 18

E. Bertino (2012) Policies, Access control and formal methods. In *Handbook on Securing Cyber-Physical Infrastructure*, S.K. Das, K. Kant, and N. Zhang (Eds.), Morgan Kaufmann, pages 573–594. Cited on page(s) 15, 16

E. Bertino and J. Crampton (2007) Security for distributed systems - foundations of access control. In *Information Assurance: Dependability and Security in Networked Systems*, Y. Qian, D. Tipper, P. Krishnamurthy and J. Joshi (Eds.), Morgan Kaufmann, pages 39–77. Cited on page(s) 16

E. Bertino and E. Ferrari (1998) Administration policies in a multipolicy authorization system. In *Proc. IFIP TC11 WG11.3 11th Int. Conf. on Database Security XI: Status and Prospects*, pages 341–357. Cited on page(s) 19

E. Bertino and G. Ghinita (2011a) Towards mechanisms for detection and prevention of data exfiltration by insiders. In *Proc. 6th ACM Symp. on Information, Computer and Communications Security*, pages 10–19. DOI: 10.1145/1966913.1966916 Cited on page(s) 45

E. Bertino and L.M. Haas (1988) Views and security in distributed database management systems. In *Advances in Database Technology, Proc. 1st Int. Conf. on Extending Database Technology*, pages 155–169. Cited on page(s) 25

E. Bertino and M. Kirkpatrick (2011b) Location-based access control systems for mobile users – concepts and research directions. In *Proc. 4th ACM SIGSPATIAL International Workshop on Security and Privacy in GIS and LBS*, pages 49–52. DOI: 10.1145/2071880.2071890 Cited on page(s) 30

E. Bertino and K. Takahashi (2010) *Identity Management: Concepts, Technologies, and Systems*, Artech House. Cited on page(s) 7, 8

E. Bertino, L.M. Haas and B.G. Linday (1983) View management in distributed data base systems. In *Proc. 9th Int. Conf. on Very Large Data Bases*, pages 376–378. Cited on page(s) 25

E. Bertino, C. Bettini, E. Bertino and P. Samarati (1998) An access control model supporting periodicity constraints and temporal reasoning. *ACM Trans. Database Syst.* 23(3), pages 231–285. DOI: 10.1145/293910.293151 Cited on page(s) 27, 29

E. Bertino, E. Ferrari and V. Atluri (1999a) The Specification and enforcement of authorization constraints in workflow management systems. *ACM Trans. Information and System Security* 2(1), pages 65–104. DOI: 10.1145/300830.300837 Cited on page(s) 51, 55

E. Bertino, S. Jajodia and P. Samarati (1999b) A flexible authorization mechanism for relational data management systems. *ACM Trans. Information Syst.* 17(2), pages 101–140. DOI: 10.1145/306686.306687 Cited on page(s) 19

E. Bertino, P. Bonatti and E. Ferrari (2001) TRBAC: A temporal role-based access control model. *ACM Trans. Information and System Security* 4(3), pages 191–233. DOI: 10.1145/501978.501979 Cited on page(s) 29

E. Bertino, B. Catania, E. Ferrari and P. Perlasca (2003) A logical framework for reasoning about access control models. *ACM Trans. Information and System Security* 6(1), pages 71–127. DOI: 10.1145/605434.605437 Cited on page(s) 36

E. Bertino, G. Ghinita and A. Kamra (2011) Access control for databases: Concepts and systems. *Foundations and Trends in Databases* 3(1–2), pages 1-148. DOI: 10.1561/1900000014 Cited on page(s) 1, 16, 61

J.W. Byun, E. Bertino and N. Li (2004) Purpose Based Access Control for Privacy Protection in Relational Databases. CERIAS Technical Report 2004-52, Purdue University, 2004. Available at `https://www.cerias.purdue.edu/apps/reports_and_papers/` DOI: 10.1007/s00778-006-0023-0 Cited on page(s) 31, 32

J.W. Byun, E. Bertino and N. Li (2005) Purpose based access control of complex data for privacy protection. In *Proc. 11th ACM Symp. on Access Control Models and Technologies*, pages 102–110. DOI: 10.1145/1063979.1063998 Cited on page(s) 31

CERT (2011) CyberSecurity Watch Survey. Data. Downloaded on April 17, 2012 from `http://www.cert.org/insider_threat/` Cited on page(s) 3

V. Chandola, A, Banerjee and V. Kumar (2009) Anomaly detection: A survey. *ACM Computing Surveys* 41(3), Article 15. DOI: 10.1145/1541880.1541882 Cited on page(s) 37

D. Cappelli, A. Moore and R. Trzeciak (2012) *The CERT Guide to Insider Threats*. Addison Wesley. Cited on page(s) 1, 2, 4

M.L. Damiani, E. Bertino, B. Catania and P. Perlasca (2007) GEO-RBAC: A spatially aware RBAC. *ACM Trans. Information and System Security* 10(1), Article 1. Cited on page(s) 30, 31

"Data, data everywhere," The Economist, 25 February 2010, Available at `http://www.economist.com/node/15557443` (Downloaded on March 30, 2012). Cited on page(s) 1

K. Fisler, S. Krishnamurthi, L.A. Meyerovich and M.C. Tschantz (2005) Verification and change-impact analysis of access control policies. In *Proc. 27th Int. Conf. on Software Engineering*, pages 196–205. DOI: 10.1145/1062455.1062502 Cited on page(s) 34

V. Gligor, S.I. Gavrial and D. Ferraiolo (1998) On the formal definition of separation-of-duty policies and their composition. In *Proc. 1998 IEEE Symp. on Security and Privacy*, pages 172–183. DOI: 10.1109/SECPRI.1998.674833 Cited on page(s) 51

M. Gelfond and V. Lifschitz (1988) The stable model semantics for logic programming. In *Proc. 5th Int. Conf. on Logic Programming*, pages 1070–1080. Cited on page(s) 55

R. Gennaro, T. Rabin, S. Jarecki and H. Krawczyk (2007) Robust and efficient sharing of RSA functions. *J. Cryptology* 20(3), pages 393–400. DOI: 10.1007/s00145-007-0201-2 Cited on page(s) 55

P. Griffiths and B. Wade (1976) An authorization mechanism for a relational database system. *ACM Trans. Database Syst.* 1(3), pages 242–255. DOI: 10.1145/320473.320482 Cited on page(s) 20, 25

US Department of Health and Human Services (2012) *Breaches Affecting 500 or More Individuals*. Available at `http://www.hhs.gov/ocr/privacy/hipaa/administrative/breachnotificationrule/breachtool.html` (downloaded on April 29, 2012). Cited on page(s) 4

M.A. Harrison, W.L. Ruzzo and J.D. Ullman (1976) Protection in operating systems. *Comm. ACM* 19(8), pages 461–471. DOI: 10.1145/360303.360333 Cited on page(s) 17

Identity Theft Center (2012) *How Burglary Can Lead to Identity Theft*. Available at `http://education.identitytheftcouncil.org/index.php?option=com_content&view=article&id=151:how-burglary-can-lead-to-identity-theft&catid=45` (downloaded on March 31, 2012). Cited on page(s) 3

A. Kamra and E. Bertino (2010) Privilege states based access control for fine-grained intrusion response. In *Proc. 13th Int. Symp. Recent Advances in Intrusion Detection*, pages 402–421. DOI: 10.1007/978-3-642-15512-3_21 Cited on page(s) 38

A. Kamra and E. Bertino (2011) Design and implementation of an intrusion response system for Relational databases. *IEEE Trans. Knowledge and Data Eng.* 23(6), pages 875–888. DOI: 10.1109/TKDE.2010.151 Cited on page(s) 38, 42, 44, 51, 55, 57

A. Kamra, E. Terzi and E. Bertino (2008) Detecting anomalous access patterns in relational databases. *The VLDB Journal* 17(5), pages 1063–1077. DOI: 10.1007/s00778-007-0051-4 Cited on page(s) 38, 39, 45

J. Karat, C-M. Karat, C. Brodie and J. Feng (2005) Designing natural language and structured entry methods for privacy policy authoring. In *Proc. Int. Conf. on Human-Computer Interaction*, pages 671–684. DOI: 10.1007/11555261_54 Cited on page(s) 33, 34

R. Kaushik and R. Ramamurthy (2011) Efficient auditing for complex SQL queries. In *Proc. ACM SIGMOD Int. Conf. on Management of Data*, pages 697–708. DOI: 10.1145/1989323.1989396 Cited on page(s) 50

M.S. Kirkpatrick and E. Bertino (2010) Enforcing spatial constraints for mobile RBAC systems. In *Proc. 15th ACM Symp. on Access Control Models and Technologies*, pages 99–108. DOI: 10.1145/1809842.1809860 Cited on page(s) 31

M.S. Kirkpatrick, M.L. Damiani and E. Bertino (2011) Prox-RBAC: A proximity-based spatially aware RBAC. In *Proc. 19th ACM SIGSPATIAL Int. Symp. on Advances in Geographic Information Systems*, pages 339–348. DOI: 10.1145/2093973.2094018 Cited on page(s) 52, 57

B.W. Lampson (1974) Protection. *Operating Systems Review* 8(1), pages 18–24. DOI: 10.1145/775265.775268 Cited on page(s) 16

W. Lee, A.C. Squicciarini and E. Bertino (2011) Detection and protection against distributed denial of service attacks in accountable grid computing systems. In *Proc. 11th IEEE/ACM Int. Symp. on Cluster, Cloud and Grid Computing*, pages 534–543. DOI: 10.1109/CCGrid.2011.28 Cited on page(s) 48

N. Li, H. Chen and E. Bertino (2012) On practical specification and enforcement of obligations. In *Proc. 2nd ACM Conf. on Data and Application Security and Privacy*, pages 71–82. DOI: 10.1145/2133601.2133611 Cited on page(s) 33

H.S. Lim, G. Ghinita, E. Bertino and M. Kantarcioglu (2012) A game-theoretic approach for high-assurance of data trustworthiness in sensor networks. In *Proc. 28th Int. Conf. on Data Engineering*, pages 120–130. Cited on page(s) 67

D. Lin, P. Rao, E. Bertino and J. Lobo (2007) An approach to evaluate policy similarity. In *Proc. 12th ACM Symposium on Access Control Models and Technologies*, pages 1–10. DOI: 10.1145/1266840.1266842 Cited on page(s) 34

D. Lin, P. Rao, E. Bertino, N. Li and J. Lobo (2010) EXAM: A comprehensive environment for the analysis of access control policies. *Int. J. Information Security* 9(4), pages 253–273. DOI: 10.1007/s10207-010-0106-1 Cited on page(s) 34, 35

J.W. Lloyd (1984) *Foundations of Logic Programming*. Springer-Verlag, New York, NY. DOI: 10.1007/978-3-642-96826-6 Cited on page(s) 54

G. Madlmayr, J. Langer, C. Kantner and J. Scharinger (2008) NFC devices: Security and privacy. In *Proc. 3rd Int. Conf. on Availability, Reliability and Security*, pages 642–647. DOI: 10.1109/ARES.2008.105 Cited on page(s) 31

S. Mathew, M. Petropoulos, H.Q. Ngo and S. Upadhyaya (2010) A data-centric approach to insider attack detection in database systems. In *Proc. 13th Int. Symp. on Recent Advances in Intrusion Detection*, pages 382–401. DOI: 10.1007/978-3-642-15512-3_20 Cited on page(s) 37, 38, 41, 42

Microsoft (2008) *Database Encryption in SQL Server 2008 Enterprise Edition*. Available at `http://msdn.microsoft.com/en-us/library/cc278098(v=SQL.100).aspx` (accessed on May 31, 2012). Cited on page(s) 61

I. Molloy, H. Chen, T. Li, Q. Wang, N. Li, E. Bertino, S. Calo and J. Lobo (2010) Mining roles with multiple objectives. *ACM Trans. Information and System Security* 13(4), Article 36. DOI: 10.1145/1880022.1880030 Cited on page(s) 35, 36

F. Monrose, M.K. Reiter and S. Wetzel (1999) Password hardening based on keystroke dynamics. In *Proc. 6th ACM Conference on Computer and Communications Security*, pages 73–82. DOI: 10.1145/319709.319720 Cited on page(s) 13

Mark Nicolett and Kelly M. Kavanagh (2011) *Magic Quadrant for Security Information and Event Management*. Gartner RAS Core Research Note G00212454. Cited on page(s) 47

OpenGIS Consortium (1999) *Open GIS simple features specification for SQL*. Revision 1.1. OpenGIS Project Document 99–049, 1999. Available at `http://portal.opengeospatial.org/files/?artifact_id=829` (Downloaded on June 2012). Cited on page(s) 30

Oracle (2012a) *Database Vault Administrator's Guide, 11g Release 1 (11.1)*. Available at `http://docs.oracle.com/cd/B28359_01/server.111/b31222/dvintro.htm` (Downloaded on May 2012). Cited on page(s) 5, 61

Oracle (2012b) *Oracle Database Security Guide 11g Release*, "Chapter 7 – Using Oracle Virtual Private Database to Control Data Access," Document B28531–16, April 2012. Available from `http://docs.oracle.com/cd/B28359_01/network.111/b28531/vpd.htm` (Accessed on May 25, 2012). Cited on page(s) 25

Oracle (20006) *Oracle Label Security Administrator's Guide, 10g Release 2*. Document B14267–02, May 2006. Available from `http://docs.oracle.com/cd/B19306_01/network.102/b14267.pdf` (Accessed on June 25, 2012). Cited on page(s) 61

Oracle (2007) *Oracle Database Vault – An Oracle White Paper*. June 2007. Available from `http://www.oracle.com/technetwork/database/security/bwp-security-db-database-vault-10gr-129787.pdf` (Accessed on May 25, 2012). Cited on page(s) 61, 62

J. Park and R. Sandhu (2004) The $UCON_{ABC}$ usage control model. In *ACM Trans. Information and System Security* 7(1), pages 128–174. DOI: 10.1145/984334.984339 Cited on page(s) 33

F. Rabitti, E. Bertino, W. Kim and D. Woelk (1991) A model of authorization for next generation database systems. In *ACM Trans. Database Syst.* 16(1), pages 88–131. DOI: 10.1145/103140.103144 Cited on page(s) 18

P. Rao, D. Lin, E. Bertino, N. Li and J. Lobo (2009) An algebra for fine-grained integration of XACML policies. In *Proc. 14th ACM Symp. on Access Control Models and Technologies*, pages 63–72. DOI: 10.1145/1542207.1542218 Cited on page(s) 35

J.H. Saltzer and M. D. Schroeder (1975) The protection of information in computer systems. In *Proc. IEEE* 63(9), pages 1278–1308. DOI: 10.1109/PROC.1975.9939 Cited on page(s) 51

E.D. Shaw, K.G. Ruby and J.M. Post (1998) The insider threat to information systems. *Security Awareness Bulletin* No. 2–98, Department of Defense Security Institute, September 1998. Available from `http://www.wrc.noaa.gov/wrso/security_guide/infosys.htm` (Downloaded on March 1, 2012). Cited on page(s) 1

V. Shoup (2000) Practical threshold signatures. In *Proc. Int. Conf. on Theory and Application of Cryptographic Techniques*. DOI: 10.1007/3-540-45539-6_15 Cited on page(s) 55

R.T. Simon and M.E. Zurko (1997) Separation of duty in role-based environments. In *Proc. 10th Computer Security Foundations Workshop*, pages 183–194. DOI: 10.1109/CSFW.1997.596811 Cited on page(s) 51

A.C. Squicciarini, A. Bhargav-Spantzel, E. Bertino and A. Czeksis (2007) Auth-SL – a system for the specification and enforcement of quality-based authentication policies. In *Proc. 9th International Conference on Information and Communication Security*, pages 386–397. DOI: 10.1007/978-3-540-77048-0_30 Cited on page(s) 8

S. Sultana and E. Bertino (2012) A comprehensive model for provenance. In *Proc. 4th Int. Provenance and Annotation Workshop*, (in print). Cited on page(s) 45

J. Vaidya, V. Atluri and J. Warner (2006) RoleMiner: Mining roles using subset enumeration. In *Proc. 13th ACM Conf. on Computer and Communication Security*, pages 144–153. DOI: 10.1145/1180405.1180424 Cited on page(s) 36

Verizon (2012) *2012 Data Breach Investigation Report.* Available at `http://www.verizonbusiness.com/resources/reports/rp_data-breach-investigations-report-2012_en_xg.pdf` (Downloaded on March 30, 2012). Cited on page(s) 1, 3

R.V. Yampolskiy and V. Govindaraju (2008) Behavioral biometrics: A survey and classification. In *International Journal of Biometrics* 1(1), pages 81–113. DOI: 10.1504/IJBM.2008.018665 Cited on page(s) 12

N. Zheng, A. Paloski and H. Wang (2011) An efficient user verification system via mouse movements. In *Proc. 18th ACM Conference on Computer and Communications Security*, pages 139–150. DOI: 10.1145/2046707.2046725 Cited on page(s) 13

Author's Biography

ELISA BERTINO

Professor Elisa Bertino is professor of Computer Science at Purdue University, where she also serves as Director of Cyber Center (Discovery Park) and Research Director of the Center for Education and Research in Information Assurance and Security (CERIAS). Her research interests cover many areas in the fields of information security and database systems. Her research combines both theoretical and practical aspects, addressing applications on a number of domains, such as medicine and humanities. Current research includes: access control systems and digital identity management; secure publishing techniques and secure broadcast for XML data; advanced RBAC models and foundations of access control models; trust negotiation languages and privacy; cloud security; and geographical information systems and spatial databases. Professor Bertino serves or has served on the editorial boards of several journals, many of which are related to security, such as the ACM Transactions on Information and System Security, the IEEE Security & Privacy Magazine, and IEEE Transactions on Dependable and Secure Computing. She served as program chair of the 36th International Conference on Very Large Data Bases (VLDB 2010) and as program co-chair of the 2011 World Wide Web (WWW'11) Conference. Professor Bertino is a Fellow of the Institute of Electrical and Electronics Engineers and a Fellow of ACM. She received the IEEE Computer Society Technical Achievement award in 2002 for outstanding contributions to database systems and database security and advanced data management systems, and received the 2005 Tsutomu Kanai Award by the IEEE Computer Society for pioneering and innovative research contributions to secure distributed systems. She is currently serving as Chair of ACM SIGSAC.

Printed in the United States
by Baker & Taylor Publisher Services